Sheryl Murphy

WHO'S DRIVING YOUR BUS?

Codependent Business Behaviors of Workaholics, Perfectionists, Martyrs, Tap Dancers, Caretakers, & People-Pleasers

Earnie Larsen
& Jeanette Goodstein

Pfeiffer
& COMPANY

Amsterdam • Johannesburg • London
San Diego • Sydney • Toronto

Copyright 1993 Pfeiffer & Company

Pfeiffer & Company
8517 Production Avenue
San Diego, CA 92121-2280 USA
(619) 578-5900   FAX (619) 578-2042

This publication is designed to provide accurate and authoritative information in regard to the subject matter covered. It is sold with the understanding that the publisher is not engaged in rendering legal, accounting, or other professional service. If legal advice or other expert assistance is required, the services of a competent professional person should be sought. *From a Declaration of Principles jointly adopted by a Committee of the American Bar Association and a Committee of Publishers.*

Editor: JoAnn Padgett
Page Compositor: Jean E. Komick
Cover: John Odam Design Associates

ISBN:
Trade Paper 0-89384-202-8
Hardcover 0-88390-372-5

Library of Congress Cataloging-in-Publication Data
Larsen, Earnie.
    Who's driving your bus?: codependent business behaviors of workaholics, perfectionists, martyrs, tap dancers, caretakers, & people-pleasers / Earnie Larsen & Jeanette Goodstein.
       p. cm.
    ISBN 0-89384-202-8 (pbk)
    1. Codependency. 2. Industrial psychiatry. I. Goodstein, Jeanette. II. Title.
    RC569.5.C63L37   1993
    158.7 – dc20   92-51019

Printed in the United States of America
1 2 3 4 5 6 7 8 9 10

For Montgomery French II,
A genius
Who has it all.

Earnie

For Len,
Without whom it could not have started
And would not have finished.

Jeanette

Contents

Preface   xi

Introduction   1

1 Behaviors and Habits: What They Are
   and How We Learn Them   7
   The Stage and the Players   8
   Relationships in Organizations   11
   Learning Behaviors and Habits   12
   Habits: What Do They Do and How?   15

2 The Bus Drivers: Behavior Patterns
   in Action   29
   Types of Self-Defeating Sets of Habits   30
   Writing Scripts, Making Tapes   39
   How It All Came to Be   41
   Bringing Our Habits to Work   44

3 The Workplace   49
   What We Bring to Work   50
   What We Find at Work   53
   Systems and How They Operate   54
   Organizational Heaven and Hell   68

4 **Codependents at Work: The Six Types in the Workplace**   **71**

Why Is Workplace Codependency So Important?   72

Codependency in the Workplace: The Six Types and Their Opposites   75

5 **Workplace Issues**   **91**

Common Themes Among the Six Types   92

The Critical Experiences—For Adults   106

6 **Workplace Implications**   **111**

How Do Your Tapes Mesh With the Organization's?   112

The Boss...and Subordinates   123

7 **Bringing the Workplace Home**   **129**

Workplace Behaviors/Family Impacts   132

Some Critical Differences Between Work and Home   139

Family Businesses   143

8 **Facing the Challenge: Change and How to Proceed**   **149**

The Experience of Change   151

Skills for Success   155

Building a Healthier Life   159

A Final Update on Our Six Friends   163

What's Next for You?   167

Index   **169**

Acknowledgments

We have a number of people to thank for their assistance and support in making this book possible. First among them is our publisher, J. William Pfeiffer, who saw the need for this book. He and Richard Roe, Vice-President for Acquisitions, were instrumental in facilitating our collaboration and developing this project. Among the many colleagues of both authors who lent their support and advice, Earnie's friend and colleague Scott Barlass deserves special mention for his review of the entire manuscript. Finally, to our editor JoAnn Padgett, who did much more than provide finishing touches, we are most grateful.

Preface

My group members had much to teach me, if only I would spend as much time listening and learning as I did being a therapist. I did pay that kind of attention to them, and they did not disappoint me. One day, much to the astonishment of all of us, a man named Pete became our teacher. Pete's attention span was nearly zero, and it was impossible for him to stay in one psychological place for more than a few minutes. Even though his body never left the group, his mind came and went regularly. You never knew when he would "disappear" or "return."

On this particular morning, Pete suddenly "appeared" and made a remarkable announcement: "I got the answer!" Since no one knew where Pete had been, let alone that there was a question, we were all curious. Well, not only did he have the answer, he even had the question and a story to go with it. Pete said, "Imagine you have a window in your forehead, so you can look in and see what's going on. There in your brain is a great big steering wheel, a big old leather seat, and even one of those hats with a badge on it—just like a Greyhound bus. The question is: 'Who's driving?' And the answer is:'I've got a hijacker driving my bus!' That's my problem, and I've got to get that hijacker out of my driver's seat." You cannot get any clearer than Pete was that morning!

Pete has plenty of company. Every one of us has one kind of hijacker or another driving our bus, at least some of the time. And maybe more than one. These bus drivers are what this book is all about: who they are, where they came from, where they are taking us, what that means for us in our lives, and what we can do about it. In the long run, being hijacked and driven off to some destination we never intended is really not wonderful. In fact, it often turns out to be really lousy. We are going to examine what happens when we surrender the wheel of our own bus, then explore what we can do about that—how we can repossess the driver's seat and once again manage our own lives.

Earnie Larsen

Introduction

The term "codependency" gets used a lot these days. It originated as a way to describe impaired (dysfunctional) relationships between alcoholics and others—the *codependents*—in their lives. In that codependent relationship, *both* people—the alcoholic and the codependent other—are trapped in self-defeating behaviors that feed on each other and are detrimental to both of them. The destructiveness of alcoholism, or any other substance abuse, both to the abuser and to family and friends, is well known to all of us. What is important to understand is that, though often related, codependency and chemical dependency are not the same thing. (Also, that changing or abandoning codependent behaviors does not necessarily cure or break a chemical dependency.)

The damage caused by codependent behavior has taken much longer to understand. Basically, the codependent person, too, has some dysfunctional behaviors. Therefore, let us say that *a codependent relationship is a destructive one in which the two people facilitate each other's dysfunctional habits.* Codependency is caused by those very self-defeating learned behaviors that diminish our capacity to initiate or participate in healthy, positive relationships. These dysfunctional behaviors are, in a way, "behavior addictions" and can be just as power-

1

ful as any substance addiction. *A behavior addiction is habitual reliance on a pattern of codependent interactions,* that is, on inappropriate ways of handling interpersonal issues. When set in motion, this pattern is very difficult to change. Because an addictive behavior is "overlearned," it is extremely difficult to "unlearn." And the mutual pattern often comes to dominate a relationship to the exclusion of other, healthy patterns.

Healthy relationships, whether between co-workers, friends, or family members, all have similar basic characteristics. The first requirement of a satisfying relationship is that each person have a solid sense of self, apart from the other. Each person must bring to the relationship adequate self-esteem and sensitivity, generally self-enhancing behavior patterns, and the ability to establish a suitable level of commitment. These characteristics will permit them to lean on each other without becoming dependent, to have differences of opinion that do not lead to win-lose situations, and to meet their own and each other's needs appropriately. As you might guess, codependents have difficulty participating in healthy relationships precisely because they lack these crucial characteristics and habits.

The first step in building healthy relationships is to look at ourselves with clear eyes and to deal with what we see. None of us, after all, is perfect. No doubt we have all picked up some habits, perceptions, and attitudes that hinder building and maintaining positive relationships in our lives. And no matter how, when, or where that happened, we need to confront them if we do not want to allow them to get in our way and to make trouble for us. As we have defined it, *codependency is our own personal unique set of patterns and habits that frustrate and obstruct our efforts to build and maintain constructive relationships with others throughout our lives—our own behavior addictions.*

These definitions focus on individuals, but it is obvious that families can become a web of codependent relationships that trap all members of a family in one way or another. Recently, many of us who study codependent relationships have reached an additional startling conclusion—all kinds of systems can be codependent, even work units, from pairs or small groups to large organizations.

Some systems are fairly simple, such as single-celled creatures or thermostats, while others, manufacturing plants or the human body, are extremely complex. Some, like thermostats, are called *closed systems* because they operate in a single loop, responsive only to internally specified signals or information. That is, only the pre-set temperatures that automatically turn heating or cooling on or off can control this system. Families or work groups, the kind of systems that we are concerned with here, are examples of *open systems*. Open systems are able to accept and respond to a wide variety of new outside information. They therefore have the ability to change and adapt to new circumstances, in contrast to closed systems, which do not. In fact, in order to function well and remain healthy, open systems need to pay attention to both their internal and external environments.

Like codependent individuals, *a codependent system is one that has developed its own unique set of patterns and habits that hinder or even prevent those who live or work in it from building and maintaining constructive relationships.* These systemic codependent patterns will typically affect both the internal and external relationships that are parts of any open system.

This discovery that systems as well as people can be codependent surely adds to the complexity of the problems that arise and makes solving them even harder. It means, for instance, that a person can have a codependent relationship with a *system,* similar to that with another person. Just think of the problems this creates. Attempting to transform a code-

pendent relationship between two people is never easy. Transformation of an entire system containing tens or even hundreds of people might seem like the work of fools, rushing in
where angels fear to tread. But we are going to try!

Do you know that *over three-quarters of all employee
terminations, firings really, at all levels are a result of personal
issues, not job competency?* And no one knows how many more
people leave their jobs because they simply can no longer
work for a difficult boss or in a "crazy" organization. Do you
also know that employee turnover costs employers millions
each year? These facts reveal that there are a lot of serious
problems around and that those problems are not "out there"
somewhere. They are right here, where all of us work and live.
These facts are worrisome to employers, to our colleagues and
friends, and to ourselves.

We believe that the vast majority of these "personal
issues" are rooted in codependency and that this statistic
about dismissals underlines the profound importance of this
problem in the workplace. This book will spotlight these
issues in order to increase our ability to understand ourselves
and those with whom we work. This understanding is useful
in its own right. But much more important for us here, it will
enhance our ability to act more effectively in the workplace
and, as a result, increase satisfaction and productivity.

Given that the first step in building healthy relationships
is self-examination, the main purpose of this book is to help
you understand what you see, both in yourself and in the
systems that you are part of. Additionally, we hope to enable
you to cope with problems you identify—whether you are an
employer, a manager, a worker stuck in an unsatisfying job or
a "crazy" organization, or someone interested in learning
more about yourself and your relationships. The key to success in handling any problems you recognize is found in four

points that must be addressed in order to build healthier relationships and a more satisfying life:

1. Grasping the patterns of our impairment (dysfunction)
2. Identifying the present consequences created by those patterns
3. Understanding that healthy functioning is the goal, that it is possible, and that reaching this goal is your own individual responsibility
4. Acquiring a support system capable of both support and challenge

Many people who enjoy happy, successful relationships do not care about and could not elucidate any of the principles embodied in this book. They are the lucky ones who do not have to. Why? They have learned and practiced the kinds of self-enhancing behaviors that are the foundation of positive, satisfying relationships. And they are aware that these behaviors are just as relevant at work as at home or at play. On the other hand, all too many others know just about everything there is to know about relationships—except how to enjoy them in their own lives. They are trapped. T. S. Eliot once wrote that "between the idea and the reality, between the motion and the act, falls the shadow." We call that shadow codependency.

If all relationships were healthy and effective, this book would not be necessary. Sadly, that is not the case. Our experience shows that codependency runs rampant in our society. We have seen that shadow at work and at school, in churches and on playing fields, in rich homes and poor ones. We have seen the costs it exacts from businesses and the havoc it plays with individuals. Millions of people are stuck in unproductive and miserable relationships. But they cannot figure out why, though they have been playing out the same old patterns endlessly, all of their lives. And millions more have to deal with these dispiriting folks, trying to figure out how to manage relationships with them at work and elsewhere without getting trapped in the same self-defeating patterns.

To lay a foundation for understanding what is happening to us and why, we must begin with a basic explanation of behavior, habits, and their developmetal process, then move on to how we use them or allow them to use us. These behaviors and habits are a large part of what we bring with us to work. Next we need to understand some things about the workplace, about organizations and systems and about what we find when we get to work. The principles contained in the next three chapters will serve as fixed points, like the stars—markers we can use to guide our progress and measure ourselves, others, and the quality of our relationships. Our relationships themselves are not built on objective principles, of course; they are based on our subjective experience of relating and of involvement. But the objective measures are important. We need them especially if we are to understand why the same things keep happening to us over and over again and how we can break that cycle.

Once we have completed these basics, we can move on to the real core of this book—codependency in the workplace and its severe negative effects, both on the organizations where we work and on us as individuals. We will conclude with an exploration of how it spills over into other aspects of our lives and the interactions that occur, what we can do about it, and how we can meet this challenge.

The bottom line of this book is really twofold. First, it addresses the challenge codependency presents to the workplace and to the bottom line there. Second, it speaks to the need in each of us to participate in healthy and satisfying relationships in all aspects of our lives. We invite you to join us in this journey of exploring ourselves and understanding others in the interest of meeting that challenge and building those relationships.

1

Behaviors and Habits: What They Are and How We Learn Them

How do you view yourself? What do you know about yourself and about your own behavior? Do you understand the effects of your actions on your co-workers, friends, and family? Are you satisfied with your relationships with your co-workers, customers/clients, and other important people in your life? Understanding yourself and others and recognizing problems of your own creation are crucial for personal and professional success. This is true whether your job is high or low in your organization's hierarchy, whether you are a business owner or self-employed.

It takes all kinds to make a world. This book is about some of these different kinds—how they behave, why, what relationships their behavior fosters, and the ensuing consequences. Although our focus is on behavior, relationships, and the consequences in the workplace, recognize that actions at work and the relationships formed there reflect how we behave and relate to others in all aspects of our lives.

The Stage and the Players

Jan, a tall, attractive, and vivacious woman in her early forties, is a first-line supervisor in a large insurance company. In managing her people she is warm and supportive, showing that she cares about each of them and views them as individuals, not just as cogs in the company's vast production machine. No matter, in fact, is too small or too personal for Jan's attention, and her ability to solve problems, or at least make things better, is legendary. Not surprisingly, her work unit has a strong sense of family, and people really enjoy working for her. On the other hand, much as they also like her, both Jan's manager and boss regard Jan's unit as the least efficient in their division. The volume of work produced by Jan's group is markedly less than that of any other similar unit, and her work unit almost never meets its production quotas or deadlines.

Chip will tell you that he has been a salesperson just about as long as he can remember. A gregarious and people-oriented person, he is a natural salesperson. Now in his thirties, Chip, who has always been popular and successful, seems to have found his place working for a business that sells or leases and maintains office equipment. Getting up to speed on the technical side of the job was easy for him. Chip looked forward to establishing long-term relationships with his customers through equipment maintenance and upgrades; he even promised to do better than his company's standard on downtime for repairs and on upgrade deals. Keeping his customers happy, though, has turned out to have some unexpected problems, and those promises often seem hard to keep.

Charles is one of the founding partners in a medical specialty practice that has grown and prospered during the last two decades. The practice has expanded to a group of six doctors, added a large support staff, and invested in sophisticated and expensive equipment required for treating patients with the latest techniques and the most advanced procedures. The partners share the tasks of maintaining their practice, managing business affairs, and supervising the staff. By unspoken agreement, Charles has become the "father" of the group. He provides medical care to the partners' families and can always be counted on to fill in for the others in a pinch. If careful records were kept, they would reveal that Charles has been "on call" for the group for far more than his fair share of holidays. And he is the one who has always worried about whether they have expanded too fast, about whether too much success would somehow spoil their practice or dilute the quality of the care they provide for their patients.

Elaine has always been known as "energetic Elaine." In school she was involved in so many activities that everyone knew her, and she even managed to hold down part-time jobs on the side. She continued this whirlwind of activity through law school without missing a beat. Nearly thirty, she is doing very well in a large law firm that is notorious for its excessive demands upon its young aspiring partners. Amazingly, she finds time for community service activities and even for her family and social life. Elaine, in other words, is one of today's young women determined "to have it all." She also epitomizes the advice, "If you really want to get something done, ask a busy person." When asked if they know how she does so much, friends or colleagues say they wish they did. But those closest to Elaine also worry that she seems unable to pause to catch her breath or to relax.

Dorothy, a woman in her late fifties and a municipal clerk in a small town, seems perfectly suited for the job she has held for nearly all her working life. Her attention to detail and insistence that "anything worth doing is worth doing right" fit neatly with a position that includes keeping minutes of all official meetings, recording and publishing city council ordinances and resolutions, and maintaining all city records according to law. Dorothy likes the orderliness required in her work and gets satisfaction from following the established routines and doing things right the first time. The standards she sets for herself are high, and she expects the same level of commitment and performance from her small staff, constantly checking their work for accuracy and timeliness. Dorothy's only disappointment, in fact, is that she is unable to find staff as committed to excellence as she is. Even those who seemed promising in the beginning either have not lived up to that promise or have not stayed for the long haul.

Jack, a rather quiet young man in his early thirties, is more adventurous than he seems at first meeting. He enjoys meeting new people, traveling, living in different places, and having challenge and variety in his work. Even during his student days, he cultivated a sense of mystery about himself and tried out different experiences by changing majors and transferring to several different schools. Artistically talented, Jack has never completely found himself and makes an adequate living as a freelance designer. This allows him to follow his instincts—some would say his whims—and indulge his desire for change and new experiences. Never married, he is an interesting and generous friend to both the women in his life and his male pals, always ready to share his limited possessions or stories of exotic places and unusual experiences. Jack's far-flung friends never know when or where he will turn up next or when he will disappear into yet another adventure.

Have you recognized yourself, co-workers, or anyone else you know among these folks? Probably. We will be encountering these players regularly throughout this book. Filling in more details of their stories will help us learn more about the impact of our own behavior in the workplace and the kinds of relationships our behavior is likely to produce.

Relationships in Organizations

How good are you at relationships? Are you able to share in healthy, productive relationships with your co-workers, your friends, and your family? Anyone who really and truly works in isolation, interacting exclusively with a computer or some other machine all day every day, can put this book aside right now. But for the 99.44 percent of us who do work with other people, our own behavior and our relationships with those people are crucial to our satisfaction and success at work.

Even though the focus of our attention is on work relationships, we will be speaking of family and social relationships from time to time as well. Why? Because we will be examining the basic *patterns* of behaviors and relationships—what works well and is self-enhancing and what does not work and becomes self-defeating. Not surprisingly, those basic patterns are common to all of our relationships. Each of us is the same person at work, at home, and at play. No one behaves in a fundamentally different way with co-workers, family, or friends.

We will be talking about how behaviors and relationships affect productivity and job performance and how they affect our sense of satisfaction in our work—about the problem of codependency and its impact in the workplace. These are the kinds of issues that lead to the majority of terminations. The personal satisfaction and success that come from doing our jobs well are, in turn, a key ingredient of the larger success of our work enterprise. They are the foundation on which productivity and profitability are built. This is true regardless of whether we are self-employed or work for a private, profit-making business where success is measured by the bottom line or whether we are working for a public sector agency or nonprofit organization where success is determined by more slippery measures of productivity and quality of service.

Now, what about relationships and behaviors? And what do they have to do with systems and organizations? At the moment we are born, we join the system that will probably have more impact on us than any other in our entire lives: our families. Most of us learn about relationships and develop patterns of behavior that will stay with us throughout our lives from our childhood experiences in our families. As we grow up, we live in a variety of systems, both in sequence and simultaneously. And we carry our patterns of behavior with us from one setting to another, from home to work to play and back again. Such patterns explain why we often find ourselves experiencing the same problems in different types of relationships and repeating certain situations in different circumstances. For example, Jack, the designer, has never stayed in any place, school, or job longer than a year. And personal relationships seems to evaporate before they settle into anything resembling a long-term commitment. Why does this pattern happen? And why does it happen again and again? Where do these patterns come from? We will explore these questions in Chapter 2.

Learning Behaviors and Habits

So who's driving your bus? These hijackers or phantom bus drivers are our old, dysfunctional habits—not just the behavior addictions that create patterns of codependency, but also those habits or patterns that push us in that direction. They are habits that we have practiced during long periods of time. We were not aware that we were practicing anything; nor, as we will soon discover, did we need to be aware. Yet practice we did, for none of us "become" anything overnight. What each one of us is today, for better or worse, is the result of behaviors that we have repeated again and again over months and years. And it is this same method—repetition and practice—that we must use to replace the hijackers in our driver's seats with new habits that are more effective and satisfying and that will drive us to a new and better destination.

Scary as it may sound, what you are or will be at sixty is what you were at thirty—doubled. No other outcome is possible, for practice makes perfect. With thirty, forty, or more years to drive the same route hundreds of times, your bus driver will be able to do it blindfolded, without even thinking about it. Habits create such mechanical reactions. And if we wish to change them, we need to understand them better.

What are habits? Where do they come from? How do we learn them? And are all of them bad? To answer the first question, habits are *patterns*—patterns of thoughts, feelings, actions, and results. While the patterns themselves are invisible, we do see the behaviors that implement them. As for the last question, of course they are not all bad. Many are, in fact, necessary to smooth functioning in our daily lives. But we will have more to say about the usefulness of habits as we consider the two middle questions: Where do they come from? How do we learn them? These require much longer answers.

Amazingly, some behaviors, like sucking, begin to emerge even before we are born! Others—grasping, crawling, and walking—emerge naturally during infancy and very early childhood. Obviously, those are not the kinds of complex, mature behaviors or habits that interest us here. We learn these complex, mature behavioral patterns through two processes that often work together.

In one of those processes, called *reinforcement*, we are praised or rewarded for doing something desirable or "good," as well as for our early awkward attempts. And, of course, we may be punished for being "bad." Reinforcement works throughout our entire lives for achievements from those as basic as cleaning our plates, hitting a baseball, or returning home at the agreed-upon time to those as complex as demonstrating systematic improvement in job performance, completing a lengthy and difficult project, or meeting sales targets.

The second process is called *modeling*. Here we observe the behavior of others and copy it ourselves. Modeling also begins at an early age and is based on the familiar examples we find around us—parents, siblings, schoolmates, teachers, fictitious characters, and so on. The old warning, "Do as I say, not as I do," proves the power of modeling. Although parents often intentionally set an example for their children, it is not necessary that they know that they are serving as a model. Nor is it necessary for someone to be aware that they are copying another's behavior. Like reinforcement, modeling is a learning process that continues throughout our lives. It is easy to see how the two processes can work together: "Watch how I brush my teeth, Susie, and do it like me. Very good!" or "Your mother will be so pleased that you are taking such good care of your cousins, Tom, just like her. You're growing up to be just as nice and thoughtful as she is!"

These learning processes guide us as we develop habits through practice. Whatever we think, feel, and do often enough becomes habit. And as adults, we have been practicing many of them for a lifetime. We have practiced these behavioral patterns so well that we have become very good at them, so good that we do not even need to think about them any more.

As helpful and effective as both these learning processes are, they do not tell us which patterns or sets of habits are healthy and constructive and which are unhealthy or dysfunctional. And you may be sure that we all have both kinds, good habits and bad ones. The good news is that once we do identify our unhealthy or dysfunctional habits, we can use these same learning processes to develop new, healthy, constructive replacements. The bad news is that doing so— abandoning old ways and adopting new ones—is not easy.

The challenges can be great and the frustrations discouraging. But there is still more good news: The struggle is worth the effort, first of all for ourselves and our future lives, and also for those we live and work and play with.

Habits: What Do They Do and How?

In general, habits make our lives easier, support us through good times and bad, and protect us from pain and discomfort. William James, America's first professional psychologist, once called habit "the flywheel of society." To serve that function and accomplish all these things, habits have four important characteristics and two broad functions.

Special Characteristics of Habits

1. *Nearly all of what we do, as much as 98 percent, results from habit, not from choice.*

   There is a very clear reason why acting out habits is not a matter of choice: *Habits operate outside of the conscious mind, where choices are made.*

   Remember that not all habits are bad. Many of our very best characteristics are also habits—self-enhancing habits. We can just leave those alone and let them continue being responsible for many of the good things in our lives. A great many other habits are neither good nor bad but simply useful. Just imagine what life would be like if you had to pay conscious attention to brushing your teeth, getting dressed, driving a car, and so on. Could you type a letter, answer the phone, and give directions to a visitor lost in the wrong office all at the same time if you had to think carefully about each element of those tasks as you did it?

Can it really be that we could be sleepwalking through our lives, not making real decisions about what we are doing? Yes, it truly can be so. And to some extent that is useful, for the ability to turn on our automatic pilots can be protective. If we were really paying attention to all of the details of our lives all of the time, we would surely suffer from severe overload. Psychological and behavioral fuses would blow more often than they do now, which is already too often for some of us. We are concerned with yet a third category of habits, the self-defeating habits that keep us from giving and receiving the best that life has to offer.

The trouble comes when we are not aware of our self-defeating behaviors. This happens when we let whoever is in the driver's seat, ourself or that hijacker, simply take the wheel and drive off with our lives. Unlearning dysfunctional behaviors demands that we be willing to put up a fight and refuse the driver's seat to bad habits—our own or those of a hijacker.

2. *Whatever we do regularly will become a habit; what we practice we will become good at.*

Generally we do not choose our habits, or at least we did not. Children are not able to distinguish between what is healthy and what is not. They simply try as best they can to get the love and acceptance that is necessary to all human beings. Chip was not aware that he was creating habits by acting out what he was taught, to work hard to please someone however he could. Chip's father was an expert woodworker. As a child, Chip tried hard to learn and succeed at woodworking, though never with much success. When did Chip start trying to please his customers the same way he used to try to please his father? And why has he let that habit overwhelm his ability to identify what he can do for customers and how long it will take?

With consistent repetition of behavioral patterns, we become very good at them. And if so much practice builds upon a natural talent, we become better than good; we can become world class! Practice really does make perfect. As we repeat a set of behaviors again and again, we no longer need reinforcement from others. We can provide it internally for ourselves. It has all become so easy. We do not have to think about what we are doing or why. We simply know on some level that we are satisfied or comfortable, or at least that we do not feel discomfort or pain.

Even adults do not always understand that a healthy habit can be carried too far and slide across the line into unhealthiness. Elaine has become so skilled at juggling activities that she probably would not know how to catch her breath if the opportunity presented itself. Even more telling, she would be so uncomfortable that she could not enjoy it. How would she know what she was supposed to do next if she had to stop, think, and choose?

3. *Habits are living things; like all other living things, they will fight to the death to stay alive.*

Most of us do not realize that when we practice a habit, we give it life. Once established, habits exist independently in our subconscious. They defend their space there and fight to stay alive, like any other living thing would do. That is why replacing an old habit with a new one is such a battle. The challenge is clear: the old habit must be killed off so that a new one can take its place.

That challenge is a serious one, not to be taken lightly or with unrealistic expectations. Unrealistic expectations quickly breed frustration and discouragement, for frustration is always tied to expectations. Our habits are truly the essence of who we are. Even their negative consequences are familiar and comfortable. It is an act of bravery to try to eliminate bad habits.

Think again about Elaine and the discomfort she would experience sitting quietly for an evening watching television with a friend or reading a book by herself. Could she even imagine relaxing for an entire weekend? Her habit of continual activity, always needing to be busy doing something—anything—has been polished to a high luster. Many admire her energy and willingness to take on new tasks. A decision to rethink her priorities and slow down would challenge her to kill off and replace a larger set of habits. It would be a truly heroic effort.

4. *Habits do not exist in isolation from one another; they are systemic,* as the preceding example illustrates so well.

They form interrelated patterns, and those patterns often join together to form large sets, or systems. These systems are, of course, open. So not only does any change in one habit affect others in its pattern or set, but the entire pattern or set can be affected by outside factors that force some kind of response. Some people seem to be very good at handling those outside factors. They are the folks we regard as flexible and open-minded, able to roll with the punches or take whatever life hands them. These are, I believe, patterns of habits that they have learned and practiced. The same is true of those we view as rigid and narrow-minded, who stick with the familiar, do not much like surprises, and cannot cope when their carefully laid plans go awry.

Let's return to Elaine, who is of the latter type. At least for now, there is virtually no chance that she will reconsider her workaholic lifestyle. But any number of outside forces could force some kind of response from her. For example, her workaholic habits are a part of what "makes" her go to work even when she is ill. She is proud of the fact that she has never taken a sick day. So imagine the impact if she were confronted by a serious accident or major illness. You can certainly begin to see how many of her habits, woven together into patterns and sets, would be forced to respond in some fashion. Or consider a different and potentially happier alternative. What if Elaine were caught unaware or actually slowed down just enough to fall in love? Such a possibility represents another kind of outside factor, but one that would provoke just as great a response.

Distinctive Functions of Habits

The first thing our habits do for us is provide the basic definitions we need to organize and understand our everyday existence. That is, *habits define both what is normal and real and what is moral.* They act like emotional glasses that we wear all the time. We see, interpret, and evaluate our reality through these glasses. Then we act accordingly.

No one really sees reality the way *it is;* instead, each one of us sees reality the way *we are.* Therefore, two people can have vastly different versions of the same incident, such as that time you were especially frazzled and one of your co-workers offered to help out but never came through. Months later, when the subject arose, you were still feeling he had let you down. But it turned out he was still confused about why you had never taken him up on his offer. Or, for another approach to reality, remember Dorothy, the municipal clerk who is committed to excellence. In Dorothy's reality, the world is full of disorder and mistakes just waiting to happen. There are mistakes lurking in the wings of all our lives, of course, but successes and other good things are waiting there too. Unfortunately, the potential mistakes are all Dorothy can see. They are her reality, her truth. They are normal.

Second, in addition to telling us what is normal, the emotional glasses provided by our habits show us what is right and wrong. They reveal our "shoulds"/"musts" and our "should nots"/"must nots." They guide us in determining what is to be judged "good" and what is to be judged "bad." Then, having brought the value judgment into clear focus, your habits determine your response. Especially in familiar situations it is not necessary to spend a lot of time or energy sorting out what is really going on and what you ought to be doing. For instance, Charles, our physician, is very clear about what is right, what his duty is, and how he must behave. Someone has to be ultimately responsible for performing the professional obligations of the practice group and, if necessary, for making whatever sacrifices are required. He is that someone.

Having defined our reality, including its moral or ethical framework, *our habits then defend that reality*. That is, they act as thermostats. There is a clear and fundamental difference between thermostats and thermometers: thermostats control the environment; thermometers simply register it. Our habits are our personal "reality thermostats." They keep our environment comfortable by ensuring that our actions match our view of what is normal and what is right. Remember that all of our habits, or sets of habits, operate without our awareness. Each has its own thermostat, set at the level that will keep us comfortable and protect us. Whenever we begin to carry out, or even imagine, new and unusual thoughts, feelings, or actions, our thermostats click into action. They control those strange impulses to make sure that we do not lead ourselves astray. In fact, what they are doing here is attempting to maintain a closed system by controlling outside forces, all toward the objective of keeping us comfortable.

These personal thermostats are ingenious and powerful. They represent our deepest selves, and that is the source of their power. The function of this subconscious self, which some call a robot and others compare to a computer program, is to judge, to assess, to make value judgments about whether a thing is healthy or not. Therefore, I call this thermostat the "guardian." Imagine Jack's guardian watching him tie himself down with too many possessions, then springing into action to guard Jack from losing his freedom to pick up and move on. Or imagine Elaine's guardian protecting her from the discomfort she would feel if she wasted an evening and accomplished nothing at all.

What regulates this thermostat or guardian? What causes it to click on, to start protecting us? Our feelings. The important thing to know about feelings is that they always face backwards; they know only what was, which behaviors feel normal and which do not. Consequently, our feelings cannot guide us to a new life. But if we are like most people, we will allow our feelings to determine how we act. Obviously, that tendency means no lasting new behavior, for establishing new behaviors and habits is uncomfortable and feels abnormal— the very things that activate our guardian.

If you want to change how you feel, you must change how you act. And you must keep at it long enough until acting in a new, more effective manner is as comfortable as acting in a self-defeating manner used to be. This is how to replace a dysfunctional habit with a self-enhancing one. And it is a formidable task!

Different results cannot come from the same old behavior; they result only from different behavior. Almost always, the obstacle to consistent and comfortable new behavior is feelings. Until you affirm and practice new behaviors and new habits long enough, until they become as much a part of who you are now as the old ones were before, you will probably feel at odds.

If our habits do indeed meet many of our daily needs and serve us so well much of the time, why or how do they turn into hijackers of our bus? First, some of them outlive their usefulness. We simply continue to use them because they are comfortable and automatic, failing to notice that they are no longer relevant. Others may not have been self-enhancing in the first place, and we will talk about some of those in the next section when we explore the origins of many of our habits. And finally, we may modify or adjust some of them little by little over time, not noticing until it is too late that what started as a self-enhancing habit has been transformed into a self-defeating one.

Where Habits Begin

Many of our habits begin at home within our families, when we are children. It is then that we have the earliest and most potent learning experiences of our lives. Understanding the processes and consequences of those experiences goes a long way toward understanding the adult each of us has become.

Healthy families raise healthy children, and healthy families provide certain essential experiences. These experiences, or family characteristics, create a positive setting for what and how children learn, the habits they develop. These characteristics are not magic bullets that guarantee perfect children or families. But we can be fairly certain that, if the characteristics are missing, problems are much more likely. These essentials include the experiences of:

- Positive predictability
- A sense of being valued and trusted
- Lasting commitments and safe touch
- Nonviolent conflict resolution
- The world as a safe place in which to live, to work, and to play

Positive Predictability

In healthy homes, children learn to expect positive situations and responses in their lives because these kinds of rewarding experiences happen predictably. Holidays are observed as joyful times, and birthdays are celebrated year after year with a party or other special event. When a child is in a school play, a sports event, or a recital, parents share in the excitement by coming to cheer the child on.

Most important of all, a healthy environment allows a child to understand that rules will be set, that consequences will be predictable and fair, that smiles will beget smiles, that a supporting hand will be there when needed, and that a child's physical and emotional needs will be met with love and affection. No parents are perfect, of course, and mistakes occur even in the healthiest of families. But expressions of positive predictability occur often enough to be counted on. They become the norm.

When positive predictability is missing, when children learn that they cannot depend on love, affection, and support, they do not develop a sense of belonging or of being connected to others. Without this sense of belonging or connectedness, the world can become an unpredictable and fearsome place where efforts to control uncertainty and establish positive predictability take top priority.

Being Valued and Trusted

Children need to learn that they are not the *only* family members who count, but they also need to learn that they *do* count. By feeling valued and affirmed, they can develop the confidence that builds lifelong self-esteem. In healthy families, children learn that there is time and space and safety for them along with other members of the family. And both boys and girls learn that there is no law against crying or expressing a full range of feelings.

Healthy environments also encourage the satisfaction of accomplishment. Children who learn that they are intrinsically valuable also learn that making mistakes does not mean that they are mistakes. Risk can be worth it, and failure need not mean disaster. In healthy families, consistent support and encouragement teach children their own value, competence, and trustworthiness.

People live up to, or down to, the expectations made of them. Since there are no perfect families, we can all remember times when we were treated unfairly as children. Some occasional bad memories are not the same as growing up in a dysfunctional family with the sense that everything was our fault, that risk inevitably led to failure, or that no effort was ever quite enough. These feelings lead children to learn that they are inadequate and incompetent, that they do not count.

Lasting Commitments and Safe Touch

Commitment means that people do not leave each other. Children come to understand that commitment and stability are normal as they see the significant people in their lives staying together. They witness people making up, saying they are sorry, and carrying on, even after an argument.

Commitment between healthy people also means that touching is safe and comfortable. By observing healthy relationships, children learn that appropriate touch is not brutal, sexual, or abusive. Children deprived of sufficient and appropriate touch will be emotionally damaged. The complete lack of touch is an especially destructive form of abuse. Research has shown that infants denied the nourishment of touch— even when they are adequately clothed, fed, and sheltered— will die.

Childhood experiences can teach that commitments do not last and that touching may not be comfortable or adequate. If important people do leave or if touching does not demonstrate commitment, children learn to fear abandonment and develop negative self-esteem. They believe that there is no other way for life to be.

Nonviolent Conflict Resolution

Healthy families tolerate and cope with anger, but not with rage. People neither lose control, hit each other, or throw things; nor do they punish, create scapegoats, or use anger as a tool to manipulate.

Children in healthy families learn that conflict does not mean an attack on personal integrity, that anger will not hurt them, and that it can be resolved through direct communication. They learn that even in the face of conflict, a safe and nurturing atmosphere can be sustained. They understand that they can live with expressions of anger and need not fear when someone "gets mad," even at them.

Violence is a learned behavior, and so are responses to violence. Violent people have almost always experienced violence as children. As either victims or as perpetrators, the patterns learned become normal. Children learn to expect beatings or other forms of abuse, and they learn to use those behaviors themselves.

The World as a Safe Place in Which to Live, to Work, and to Play

Play is the work of children. Play is also a part of the lives of healthy adults, and healthy families play together. But play requires a world that is safe, where play may be given its proper importance and where children can learn to play. Our world today has too many unsafe places—urban ghettos, countries torn by civil war, refugee camps—where circumstances do not allow a playful childhood.

Even in safe settings, children also need to learn that play, like other aspects of life, has limits. Even for children, play must be suitably balanced against other work, especially the work of formal learning. Priorities must be made. Play is not appropriate when there is other work to be done. The middle of the harvest season is no time for a vacation, nor is the middle of the school year. But healthy lives allot time for play; work is not the sole priority. When life is all work, or when the fundamental task is basic survival, children never have the opportunity to learn to play. If the child does not learn how to play, the adult knows only how to be serious.

To summarize, we can put these five critical experiences and their effects into a chart:

CRITICAL EXPERIENCES	RESULT IF PRESENT	RESULT IF MISSING
• Positive Predictability	Sense of belonging	Sense of alienation, high need for control
• A Sense of Being Valued and Trusted	Sense of achievement	Sense of shame or guilt
• Lasting Commitments, Safe Touch	Ability to trust	Fear of abandonment, negative self-esteem
• Nonviolent Conflict Resolution	Search for nonviolent solutions	Rely on violence or become a victim
• World Safe for Life, Work, and Play	Playful spirit	Excessive seriousness

Healthy families create positive environments. They enable their children to learn, to practice healthy habits, and to mature into healthy, happy, and productive adults. Dysfunctional families create environments in which children learn and practice unhealthy, even destructive habits. Carrying such habits with them into adult life, some of these individuals are severely maladjusted and lead very unhappy, disturbed lives. Others may not be so severely damaged, but find their lives less satisfying and productive than they could be.

Though our family provides our first and most important learning environment, other influences also contribute. Movies and television are notorious for emphasizing violence as the way to resolve conflict, and researchers have demonstrated the powerful effects on children of watching so much violence. School, where we spend about a quarter of our time as children and teenagers, teaches more than the three R's. It also presents opportunities for learning behaviors and habits. The shy or unpopular child who is always the last to be chosen for any team or activity does not feel valued. Children who do well and who like school will experience positive predictability in their school environment and the sense of acceptance and belonging that it builds. No doubt you can think of many more happy and painful examples. Even as we become adults, these types of critical experiences continue their importance in our lives, so we will be returning to them from time to time and will reassess them in terms of workplace needs and conditions.

Wherever it comes from—home and family, school and teachers, friends or other people, or circumstances—all of this experience and learning and practice has a purpose: to guide and shape our behavior in ways that feel comfortable and produce satisfying results. The learning that begins in childhood may or may not produce lifelong comfort and satisfaction. The result depends both on what we have learned and on how we are using it.

2

The Bus Drivers: Behavior Patterns in Action

Y ou probably can already think of many examples of simple habits and behavioral patterns in your own life and in the lives of others. Some are useful or enhance our lives—the sales rep who always brings along a box of donuts, the boss who remembers to say "well done!" when it is deserved, the colleague who can be counted on in a pinch. Others are self-defeating and reduce effectiveness—the co-worker who dominates meetings by interrupting anyone and everyone, the supervisor who criticizes publicly, the excessively demanding client. These patterns get in the way of both the person who acts those habits out and those who find themselves on the receiving end.

But what about more complex patterns? The kinds of behavior patterns described in the six vignettes at the beginning of this book. Are those habits too? They surely are. They are large sets of habits, made up of any number of related habits that join together into an open "system" of habits. They are learned the same way that simpler habits are. And like them, these large sets of habits may be constructive or destructive. But unlike the simpler ones, because of their size and complexity, these sets are even more firmly rooted in our subconscious. They may not be harder to identify, but they are certainly more difficult to kill off.

Types of Self-Defeating Sets of Habits

The six vignettes represent six categories of self-defeating habit sets. While you may think of some additions or variations, these categories cover a lot of common, habitual, and codependent patterns. It is true that you can get trapped in these self-defeating habits by yourself. You do not have to play them out exclusively in a codependent relationship. But it is also true that we often do look for, and find, someone whose own dysfunctional habits match our own. *When both people bring matching dysfunctional habits to a relationship, the possibilities for disaster multiply. And when the matching partner is not an individual person, but an organization—and we will explore that prospect in a later chapter—those possibilities multiply yet again.*

Each of the six types is intentionally described in extremes to dramatize the issues each presents. Even if any one type with all its characteristics is not a perfect fit, you may recognize some fragments of yourself, or people you know. And many people, including us, recognize aspects of themselves in more than one category.

Caretakers

On the surface, Caretakers dedicate their lives to taking care of others. But they do more than that, for the bottom line for

Caretakers is really control. For whatever reasons, Caretakers have become obsessed with the need to maintain as much control as they possibly can over their environment. Above all, they do not like surprises. Consequently, they attempt to take control of those around them and to breed dependency. Caretakers presume to know the needs of others without consulting them, as well as the exact methods to satisfy those needs. And having honed their skills in dominating the people and circumstances of their lives, Caretakers have also learned to base their self-image and sense of accomplishment on their ability to do things for other people.

Since all relationships are two-way streets, Caretakers need people around them who are dependent, who want to be cared for. If there are not any dependent people around, Caretakers will have to find some or create some if they must, making people into "babies" in order to satisfy their habit and their self-esteem. The dependency may be physical, requiring the Caretaker to provide food, clothing, shelter, or transportation. Or it may be psychological dependency, such as needing the Caretaker to make decisions, to approve choices, to give support, and so on.

If all this caretaking sounds too good to be true, it is! For both the Caretakers and those they care for, their babies. This may resemble the normal dependency of children or the elderly, but make no mistake—it is dysfunctional and, therefore, it is different. The dependent babies may learn that they never really have to take responsibility for themselves or their actions. Why? Because their Caretaker will be there for them, to fix whatever needs fixing, to make things right, to bail them out, to make them feel better.

Caretakers, in turn, may find themselves overwhelmed by the needs of the babies they have encouraged. "There's not one responsible person in my life!" they complain. "What about my needs?" Well, of course. Taking care of the needs of others can become a demanding occupation and leave no time for one's own needs. And focusing all of one's attention on the needs of others can make it easy to ignore important issues such as loneliness or personal or job dissatisfaction. But Caretakers *can* learn to stop taking control and playing God and allow others to take responsibility for themselves.

The Caretaker-Baby relationship is an especially clear example of codependency, for their need for each other is so clear. A Caretaker can, of course, attempt to smother anyone available; and a Baby can try to hand over responsibility to whoever is handy. But the natural fit is obvious. So are the opportunities for each to reinforce the dysfunctional habits of the other. Later, we will identify opposites or matches for each of the other types, but for now let us focus our attention on our primary types as we continue.

People-Pleasers

People-Pleasers have not learned how to say no. What they have learned is how to avoid causing another person to be angry, unhappy, or inconvenienced. Their motto is "Don't rock the boat!" and the point of this behavior is to make sure that people will continue to like them. The fact that they are giving away their power is far less important than their fear that saying "no" would cause others to get mad and turn away. If that happened, it would just prove that they really are bad and that others will surely go away and leave them alone permanently.

To avoid this potential disaster, People-Pleasers learn to do just what their label proclaims, please others. They are always likeable and usually very charming; they are always agreeable and often go out of their way to be helpful. They are always cooperative, but regularly promise more than they can deliver. And along the way they also learn to pretend; to evade, even to lie to protect and please others, not themselves.

Emotional dishonesty becomes a way of life for them. When asked how their day has gone, they will invariably respond, "fine," no matter how lousy it has been. Or when asked about some choice, they will say, "Whatever you want is fine with me," regardless of how strong their preferences may be.

The problem is that People-Pleasers are not fine. They do not receive enough of the basic friendship and the emotional or moral support we all need because they do not say when they are angry, stressed, disappointed, or whatever. To do so, they fear, would put their relationships in jeopardy. But *not* to do so keeps their own needs and feelings secret and often leads to misunderstandings or worse. People-Pleasers unrealistically hope that others will somehow intuitively know what they do not say and then come through with the professional, personal, or social responses they seek. But all too often those hopes are dashed, and People-Pleasers wind up feeling unsupported, abandoned, and hurt. They are always in a state of emotional starvation. And while they are starving, they indirectly punish the others for not giving what they did not ask for.

These behavior patterns often lead People-Pleasers into exploitive or even abusive relationships. People who are willing to surrender their power often attract others who are willing to take that power and use it for their own advantage. People-Pleasers' fear of offending outweighs the value they place on their own needs or on themselves. They need to learn to assert their own legitimate rights without feeling apologetic and unworthy. They can learn to say, "I count!"

Martyrs

Martyrs are pessimists through and through. They have learned that when things are going too well, trouble is brewing. Actually, even when trouble is already here, *more* trouble is brewing. Pain is normal. And pain is reassuring, because for all of us anything other than normal is frightening. Martyrs understand that life is a serious responsibility and not meant to be *too* good; the key to getting through it is basic endurance and acceptance of their own lack of worth. Consequently, life has meaning only when it is filled with struggle and suffering. Nothing is ever really good, genuinely pleasing, a pure joy—except, perhaps, the struggle.

Convinced of their own unworthiness, Martyrs believe that they have no right to a share of life's goodies. As a result, they fear both success and pleasure and go out of their way to avoid them. When life is going along too smoothly, Martyrs find ways to create havoc. Doing so is one of their great skills, and they work hard at it. Their weapons of choice are the twins—worry and guilt. Worry makes sure that today is not too good. When they have reached their limit and worried enough about their job security, their children's grades, and their retirement plan, they can always take on the the world's problems—war in the latest hot spot, global warming and pollution, and so on.

Guilt can lay a widespread and long-lasting pall, as Martyrs do their best to dampen the enthusiasm, optimism, and fun of those around them. When the celebration becomes too joyous, the Martyr will interject a somber reminder of those no longer with us to share the occasion. Or instead of congratulating a colleague on a promotion, the Martyr will remark upon the demands of the new position and the family sacrifices that will be required. Part of their responsibility, after all, is to impress upon their lighthearted colleagues and family members the seriousness of life. All else failing, Martyrs can induce their own guilt simply by reviewing, yet once more, their own flaws and failings.

Martyrs embrace and cause hurt and pain, then explain it as "God's will" or "destiny." They, too, can break their old habits and be reborn. They will probably never become totally footloose and fancy free, but Martyrs can certainly learn to stop interfering with other people's happiness, and they can try to learn to enjoy life's simple pleasures.

Workaholics

Workaholics need to be active and busy, all the time. Most people think that Workaholics base their self-esteem on productivity and achievement, and that foundation is true of some of them. They are professionally respected and admired for both their successes and the energy that drives them. But if you pay closer attention, you will also notice many Workaholics who simply must be busy, whether or not they actually accomplish anything. Continual motion seems to be the point for these folks, and they sometimes seem to be genuinely ambivalent about productivity and achievement. Completing a task or a project, you see, might leave them without anything to do. Some Workaholics are obviously better than others at keeping a steady array of future projects lined up and ready to go.

Whichever type they are, all Workaholics are driven by the same basic belief—projects and activity take top priority, ahead of people. They often seem to act as if the people in their lives are an inconvenience and not an essential part of a healthy, balanced life. And they often have little patience for human frailties or flaws, especially what they regard as a lack of discipline or conscientiousness on the part of others who do not share their workaholism. This willingness to put work or activity ahead of people is the primary thing that separates the true Workaholic from other hard workers. It also explains the underlying problem of Workaholics—their fundamental loneliness. Unwilling, or even afraid, to let others too far into their lives, they keep busy as the only way they know to push back their loneliness. This distancing behavior, in turn, pinpoints the second distinguishing factor of a true Workaholic, the inability to relax. Though they have learned too well how to stay busy, they have never learned how to unwind and take it easy.

Workaholics seem easy to identify, though we should not confuse them with people who know how to work hard and play hard in a healthy fashion. One clue of the inability to relax is the person who seems to turn even play into work. Another is visible in those "indispensable" people whose jobs expand to fill evenings and weekends. Or for the equally indispensable wife and mother who has gotten carried away with "a woman's work is never done." Being regularly employed is not a requirement for being a Workaholic, though it does make it easier.

Workaholics need their "busyness" to maintain their self-esteem and to hide their loneliness. Activity—even when it yields money, prestige, and things—cannot fill the void they feel inside. Only learning how to build relationships and let other people in will do that. To achieve that goal, the Workaholic also needs to learn to relax and to understand that taking time to smell the flowers and watch the sunset restores and replenishes the spirit. It is possible to fill the void.

Perfectionists

Pity the poor Perfectionist! Since nothing in this life can ever be perfect, Perfectionists can never be happy or satisfied. They must always do more and better, for their dedication to quality performance and products exceeds all reasonable bounds. Perfectionists typically claim that they simply want things to be "good enough." Unfortunately, for them, "good enough" means "perfect" because their self-esteem is always on the line. Over time they have learned to drive themselves unmercifully in an attempt to match their elusive and unattainable ideals.

Not only are Perfectionists themselves to be pitied, but also those who live and work with them merit our sympathy. Perfectionists generally apply their impossible standards to the people and things around them as well as to themselves. They are, after all, expecting no more of others that they expect of themselves. They have honed their skills in recognizing imperfection, commenting on it, and allowing it to dominate their lives. And, of course, they do not have far to look in their search to identify and root it out, since nothing is ever really good enough. A top-producing team, which had also exceeded quality targets in five consecutive periods, finally was narrowly beaten out by its closest rival, only to hear from the Perfectionist boss, "Well, how soon are you going to get your performance back up to an acceptable standard?" Living with a Perfectionist, whether at home or at work, can become a frustrating and degrading exercise in futility.

Perfectionists can rarely maintain satisfying and effective relationships with the others they subject to their intense scrutiny and unrealistic expectations. They wonder why those others are so inattentive to detail, so sloppy, so oblivious to the importance of quality. When they can, they will require that the work be redone. And even when they do not have the authority to do that, they often find it difficult to bite their tongues and refrain from commenting. As a result, they often find themselves increasingly isolated in a sterile and solitary world of fault finding and blame. Sadly, their relationship with themselves is often not much more satisfactory, for they must often point that finger at themselves. Perfectionists need to come to terms with an imperfect world and to base their self-esteem on achievable standards. They need, in other words, to learn to accept themselves as they are, warts and all. And they need to allow others the right to their own faults and foibles as well. The result will be lives that are richer and more satisfying.

Tap Dancers

Tap Dancers are so terrified of commitment that they have learned how to avoid it under almost any circumstances and at almost any cost. How do they do this? It is easy if you never stand still, at least not emotionally. Their constant motion is the source of their name. When things start getting serious, Tap Dancers will not give a straight answer. They are all experts at slipping out through back doors.

Though their main fear is usually of long-term or permanent personal relationships, the anxiety of Tap Dancers often spills over into other areas of their lives. They may hop from job to job or move restlessly from one apartment to another. They may pride themselves on having hardly any possessions and on being able to pick up and go. Stability, they say, is boring; but, in fact, that is not the real issue. Tap Dancers are not truly seeking change for its own sake or new experiences as they claim. Instead, they are running away from relationships or commitments. Staying in one place—with one job, one set of friends, one primary relationship—risks letting others come to know them too well. So Tap Dancers give enough to keep another person on the string, but never enough to really grasp and hold on to. They never permit the expectations they generate to come to fruition.

When a personal relationship reaches the point of commitment, when a boss begins to project responsibilities and rewards into the long-term future, a Tap Dancer retreats in a panic. The excuses offered often sound reasonable but do not stand up to close examination. Tap Dancers are experts at the half-truth or the veiled truth. Underneath lies the fear of commitment and the risk of being found out—the discovery that they offer less than meets the eye. Life becomes a game of hide-and-seek, one in which Tap Dancers make sure never to be found.

Behind this fear or determination never to be found out is a deep sense of inadequacy. A Tap Dancer is certain that "If anyone really knew me, they would know that I am a fraud, an empty shell. They could see right through the person they think they know and would never have anything more to do with me." For Tap Dancers, the best way to avoid rejection is to avoid serious relationships in the first place and never allow them to get off the ground. Tap Dancers need to learn to stand still and to value themselves. Once they understand that commitment can bring freedom and satisfaction—and, above all, acceptance—they can also come to realize that it is not always painful and stifling.

If a sense of recognition has mushroomed into desperation while working through these types—"My God, I'm all of them"—don't despair! Remember that no one is perfect, and that each of us probably has some bits and pieces of all these patterns in our lives. But this raises important questions: What do we do with these habits and patterns? How much power do we allow them in our lives? Do you let them drive your bus?

Writing Scripts, Making Tapes

There are set sequences of behaviors that we use without thinking or even making a conscious choice, as if they were tapes that run from start to finish when they are switched on. They are so automatic, in fact, that they are often nearly impossible to interrupt. Once they are firmly recorded and set in play, basic changes are rare—though they may generate new, revised versions to fit changing life circumstances. Like our habits, some of our tapes are self-enhancing, some are simply useful, and some are self-defeating. Some, as we are about to see, are the mechanisms we use to act out the dysfunctional types just described.

By now, you will surely recognize this kind of situation. For example, on a Friday morning Charles, the physician—

you can identify him now as the Martyr type—is accosted in his office by a colleague who explains an unexpected family situation and asks whether Charles could please take call for him this weekend. Charles responds that he has promised his own wife that he will try not to work so hard (remembering also how she complains about the group's members taking advantage of him). The colleague counters with how he, too, has promised to spend more time with his wife and children, so he does understand, but that this is a family matter, and so on. The upshot is that, as usual, Charles can be counted on to come to the rescue. The tape has played again, with only the most minor variations in the script followed by both Charles and his colleague.

We all have hundreds of these tapes standing by, cued and ready to play. Stop and think for a minute about your own life, at work and at home. No doubt you can easily think of several of your own tapes that you run regularly, as well as those of others that you play a role in. Many of these scripts and tapes have their origins in our childhoods, where they once served some useful purpose in our lives. Others may be new versions or adult adaptations of scripts that were set years earlier. Even as a teenager, for instance, Charles was already putting aside his own needs and desires in favor of his widowed mother and younger sisters. The one played out with his colleague on that Friday morning is simply the adult workplace version of the tape that originated in the context of family relationships when he was a teen. And, as you might imagine, he has an updated family version now as well that includes his wife and children.

One of the most important things about these scripts and tapes is that, though they rarely change, they do not all live on actively forever. Some fade out naturally, and appropriately, as we outgrow them.

We also all know people who continue to use old tapes that have outlived their usefulness. A good friend of mine, a successful athlete, was also an excellent student who went on to a doctorate in economics and a career as a professor. From the time of his early achievements, he was regarded as a very promising young man. The day finally came when he was not so young any more; in fact, by fifty he was a bit too old to still be considered "promising." But he was still relying on his old tape, playing it until it ran out and failing to notice that it had stopped. He postponed growing up until it was too late.

How It All Came to Be

Like people's tapes, our six self-defeating types have their origins in childhood learning. They grow from the need of every child for love and affection, approval, and validation. People who exemplify each of the types do not spring magically into full bloom as adults. For years they have *practiced* becoming who they are.

Learning begins at an early age. Children are reinforced for their early and sometimes awkward attempts at caretaking, at working hard and doing a good job, at pleasing those whose love and approval they need. They also model the behavior of those significant people. Children learn from negative experiences as well as the positively reinforced ones. A child who has lost a parent, for whatever reason, may learn to fear abandonment and then to avoid commitments. Another child may have a parent who might as well be truly gone, perhaps because that parent is a Workaholic or an alcoholic. This child, too, may learn some of the behaviors of the Tap Dancer, or alternatively, learn to be a Workaholic or even an alcoholic! The child of a Perfectionist may endure the frustrating experience of trying harder and harder to please someone who, in the end, can never be fully pleased. If not learning to be a Perfectionist, this child may develop into a first-class People-

Pleaser. The possibilities, as you can see, are many and varied. But before these scenarios begin to sound like laying all the blame on our parents, we had better slow down and consider some other possibilities.

First of all, many behaviors, like many good foods, are often healthy in reasonable quantities. It is only overindulgence that creates problems. The nurturing habits of Caretakers, the quality standards of Perfectionists, the social skills of People-Pleasers, and so on can all be self-enhancing. *They do not become dysfunctional until they are carried to extremes.* The problem here is how to tell when a positive, self-enhancing habit or pattern slips across the line and becomes excessive and codependent. Unfortunately, no early warning system alerts us to the danger of that hijacking bus driver who is about to slide into our driver's seat.

The problem becomes even trickier when we realize that our strengths contain the seeds of potential weakness. What do I mean by this? We tend to use our strengths—our skills, talents, things we are good at—often for they are positively reinforcing. So, the more we do them, the better we become and the more reinforcement we receive. And, the more likely we are to slide over the line into excess. Imagine a rather serious child being rewarded for behaving responsibly, then being given more responsibility, and finally assuming more and more responsibility for both people and events until becoming a full-fledged Martyr. You can see how something similar could happen with each one of our types.

A few pages ago we observed that one thing that distinguishes a Workaholic from a healthy hard worker is the inability to relax. This is a subtle sign, but one you can identify if you look for it. Similarly, Caretakers not only take care of the needs of others, they define those needs for them. If you have been acquainted with any Tap Dancers for a length of time, you have probably learned how to tell when you, or anyone else, pushes too close. Sometimes they withdraw psychologically; at other times they may literally disappear for weeks or more. In other words, the signs are there; but you do have to pay attention, for codependency is a stealthy conspirator. Codependency, let alone the extremes represented by the six types, does not happen overnight. It is part of a cycle that begins with the initiation of behavior, continues with years of training and practice, and carries on with the training of others.

But this cycle can be broken. Sometimes, as with some tapes, we outgrow certain habits or patterns. As we move on to new stages of our lives, our experiences change. We may not even have to think about the need to discard some behaviors. It is also true that codependency does not necessarily infect absolutely all of our life and behavior. Sometimes it involves only certain types of relationships or situations—perhaps with a boss that reminds us, even if unconsciously, of a parent, or in a work group where we assume the same role we did among the close group of friends we grew up with.

So what about our parents' place in that cycle? They did not invent the dysfunctional behaviors or habits that they act out in their own lives or that they reinforce in ours. They learned and practiced them in the same ways that we have. No matter where and how the cycle began, it can be broken. With effort, we can break it in our own lives, and we can avoid carrying it on or teaching these same self-defeating habits to our own children.

We also need to remember a couple more things, both about our parents and the origination of these habits, and about ourselves and the possibility that we may be teaching them again to a new generation. One is that parents are not the only reinforcers. There are many more out there in life—teachers, school, friends, cultural icons, church, and so on. Though parents are the first and most powerful teachers, all of these others become more and more important as children grow older. One example is how Christianity, and especially the Protestant work ethic, reinforces the habits that can create a Workaholic.

The second thing to remember is that parents—or others, including ourselves—do not always reinforce or model what they think they are. A mechanical drawing student, the son of some friends, was assigned to draw a floor plan and chose my house as his model. The completed drawing looked very neat, but the plan was not accurate. When I asked, he said, "Well, my measurements were not correct, so I just added this room here to make it all come out right." His father complimented the drawing without commenting on the "adjustment" in the plan. Now I know that his father values integrity and lives it in his own life. His father thought he was reinforcing the drawing and homework. What he failed to recognize was that he was *also* reinforcing the idea that it is all right to misrepresent things a little, so long as the result looks fine.

Bringing Our Habits to Work

As you can see, we all bring a great deal of what we began learning as young children into adulthood with us. And we bring it into all aspects of our adult lives. Just because we began training in our habits at home and school does not mean that they are limited to our personal or social lives. We all bring them to work with us, too.

Bringing these self-defeating habits along to work does seem a little surprising when you first think about it. After all, many of us think that we behave differently at work than in the rest of our lives—that the gap between these two areas is large and rarely bridged—because the activities seem to be so different. Yet once you begin to get used to the idea, it is not surprising because the underlying patterns of behavior remain constant. When the Workaholic goes home, it is simply to a different list of projects. And though the Perfectionist may know how to relax, you can bet that as much energy goes into perfecting a golf swing or tending rose bushes as into balancing the quarterly report figures.

To end this chapter, let's preview some of the negative effects these behaviors have in the workplace—how these habits and dysfunctional types of behavior get in our way and how they can cause damage. We will focus our attention on cooperation and teamwork because they are crucial to success in virtually all organizations and have become a center of attention in our increasingly competitive marketplace. These are also good choices because teams, like families, are a network of relationships, and relationships can be only as healthy as the people involved. An effectively functioning team will outproduce a bickering lot of distrustful egocentric superstars every time! All too often, however, this growing emphasis on team building is based on the assumption that team members already have the skills and abilities they need, that "Of course this group can function as a true team if the members have a few pointers on how to proceed." This assumption is false. Dropping in on our six initial friends will show us why and how.

You have, no doubt, identified Jan as a Caretaker. Though she is nice, supportive, and well-liked, she has enormous difficulty letting others grow up, make mistakes, and take responsibility (with all the blame or glory that must accompany that responsibility). While she thinks that she is their best friend, protecting them from their flaws and faults, she is actually their worst enemy as she attempts to turn them all into her babies. No matter how many resources are committed to team building, Jan's group will never be as successful as it could be because she cannot tolerate a genuine team. Jan cannot even view herself as a leader who is first among equals.

She must create a dependent family that clusters around her, the overprotective mother hen.

Chip is our People-Pleaser—a nice guy and good sales-man who is always positive and full of energy. Yet team building, like family building, depends on honesty and truth, not on promises that sound good but cannot be kept. Chip does not hesitate for a moment to tell people what they want to hear, even when he knows that his promises are unrealistic and that he can't deliver. The extent to which Chip can be part of a team is limited at best, for no one will fully accept an untrustworthy team member. As "nice" as People-Pleasers seem to be, they simply cannot be trusted. And it does not take long for others to discover that untrustworthiness, either by being burned themselves or by watching it happen to someone else.

Charles, of course, is a Martyr. It is not that he is always down in the dumps, unhappy, or a walking case of clinical depression. He is not. Generally, he does not have time for any of those feelings. He is too busy making sure that everything is properly taken care of, worrying whether the success of their practice will damage the quality of care they provide, sacrificing himself for the sake of the common good. He is too busy to be anything but ever vigilant. Obviously, team building is not important simply for the sake of having a team. It is critical for the sake of accomplishing identified ends, and those ends include not only the work or tasks of the team but also the mutual support and celebration of the smooth-functioning and accomplished team. Martyrs short-circuit this rejoicing every time. They are not able to see the sunshine for the few scattered clouds on the horizon.

To know Elaine, the Workaholic, is to marvel at and even applaud her achievements. As much as Workaholics accomplish personally, they are the wrecking crews of morale. Defining themselves by the amount of work they perform, they have no boundaries dividing what they need to do from what others must accomplish. And since they often sport a large dash of perfectionism, they place unreasonable quality as well as quantity demands on those around them. Simple common sense dictates how devastating Workaholics are to teams, for true teams display mutual admiration and respect. Since others seldom work long enough, hard enough, or well enough to suit the Workaholic, mutual admiration and respect are in short supply. The reaction of those who experience the whip of the Workaholic is more likely to be a mutiny than a commitment to team effort.

Dorothy, with her motto of "If it is worth doing, it is worth doing right," is a model Perfectionist. There is nothing wrong with the pursuit of excellence; rather, it is the expectation of perfection that causes problems. Even though perfection is not possible, Perfectionists are absolutely intolerant of imperfection. Nothing is ever done fast enough or well enough; or nothing is prepared in the proper quantity. It is not possible for anyone, including Perfectionists themselves, to live up to such demands. Obviously, they are not happy people or very easy to be around; so when it comes to teamwork, the Perfectionist is a real detriment. After all, who wants to be around someone who cannot be pleased, who constantly exudes a sense of disappointment with any and all efforts, and who simply cannot be satisfied? Such a person weighs down a team like a cannonball would weigh down a long-distance swimmer.

Finally, we get to Jack. Like most Tap Dancers, he is interesting and fun to be around. He is like a bird out of a cage; you never know where he is going to alight, or even if he is going to show up. But also like all Tap Dancers, he puts out a message that shouts, "It is not safe to get too close!" Their glamorous mystique is typically accompanied by the sense that they are not willing to lay all their cards on the table and that you cannot count on them when the chips are down. They seem to have some inner mechanism that constantly demands change to keep them from feeling penned in. Tap Dancers just do not cut it when it comes to team building and teamwork. They are loners; when they begin to feel suffocated, they take off—emotionally, if not physically. Their lack of reliability and commitment to their colleagues is self-evident, as is their effect on any team unlucky enough to have to work with them.

Now, a last reminder before we plunge into an exploration of the workplace and then on to the detrimental result of codependency: no one is perfect. All of us face some of these obstacles. In fact, we each probably have a little bit of all these patterns in us. It is just a matter of degree. That does not mean that we are "sick." The basic point is not to see how broken we are. The point is that we can deal with anything we can recognize and call by name. If we cannot label these patterns, we will find it very hard to recognize them or be aware of them. And if we are not aware of them, they will continue to create trouble in our lives. But if we can identify these obstacles, we can also begin to understand them and work through them to more satisfying and effective ways of working, playing, and living.

3

The
Workplace

What does being "grown up" mean? Are you mature? How do you know? Many youngsters think that those concepts are the same and that they will be grown-up when they have a job and a family.

This child's view, although simplistic, is not so far off. Someone once asked Sigmund Freud what signified genuine maturity. His answer was brief and direct: love and work. Truly mature people are, by definition, generally satisfied with their lives and their families, effective in what they do in both their work and leisure time, comfortable with the tapes they retain and continue to use, balanced in their outlook, and content with themselves. Knowing how to love and how to work, they truly do know how to live. We would add that they also know how to play. And they do these things successfully most of the time. But "successfully" does not mean free of problems. It does not mean a perfect record or even a long streak of successes. And it does not mean that their road toward maturity was an easy one. It does mean perseverance and a continuing search.

Maturity is an important goal for all of us, and it is one we can all achieve—even though it often seems especially elusive if we are entangled in the traps of codependency. Achieving maturity, however, is no guarantee. We must value it and maintain it. The process of reaching the goal takes longer for some of us than for others and, for some, getting there is *not* half the fun.

In any case, one of the most important things to remember is that getting there is a process, a continuous one. Another is that the opposite of mature is immature, not sick. Starting from Freud's definition of maturity, we recognize that codependency is one of the characteristics of immaturity. It interferes with both loving and working. Immaturity is not a disease to recover from, it is a stage that we must all pass through—hard as that may be for parents of adolescents to believe! Maturity is a state that we can all grow into. It is the goal to strive for.

What We Bring to Work

We bring ourselves, of course. But what exactly is that? Does that self that goes to work include only those parts relevant to the job? Of course not. The self that goes to work is the whole package. It includes all the strengths you have developed—presumably the reasons you were hired. These probably consist mainly of your education, experience, and technical or job skills. To these, add other strengths that may or may not turn out to be relevant. Your athletic ability might win you a place on the company team; a job or organizational change might suddenly make your knowledge of a foreign language significant.

That is all the good stuff, but the truth is that we also bring our warts and weaknesses along with us too. Like our strengths, our weaknesses also vary in importance. A gap in job skills requiring additional training might be balanced by exceptional abilities or experience in another aspect of the job. Not being a good athlete or not even wanting to join the sports program probably does not matter at all.

In addition to these various strengths and weaknesses, we also bring our behavioral habits and patterns—all of those scripts and tapes that we have spent a lifetime learning and practicing. There is virtually no job that is fully isolated from co-workers, customers/clients, or other human contact. And there is no earthly reason to think that the interpersonal skills we bring with us—our patterns and habits—will be different at work from those we brought in the past or those we leave home with every morning. Those that have been healthy and self-enhancing will continue to be, supporting us at work just as they do at home and at play. Those that are self-defeating will be just as damaging to our effectiveness and satisfaction at work as they are elsewhere. In fact, most studies show that at least 85 percent of people fired from their jobs are dismissed because of their interpersonal limitations. It is their inability to get along with others—co-workers, bosses, subordinates, customers—not poor technical skills that is the cause of their troubles. And this statistic is true at all organizational levels.

You cannot switch off your Caretaker habits or replace your Martyr tape—or any of the others—for a few hours on certain days of the week. The only ways we know how to relate to others are the ones that we have practiced and learned so well that we do them without thinking. Our designer Jack started learning to fear commitment, and intimacy, a long time ago—his father had a breakdown when Jack was only five. From that experience, Jack learned self-reliance; he could not count on others. Dependence of any sort became a "no-no" for him; his motto became "do it yourself." This learning became the core of his set of Tap Dancer behaviors, later supplemented by his desire for change and new experience.

Because he is a talented designer, Jack has had several excellent opportunities for good jobs. He never even seriously considers them and turns them down almost automatically, even when he has no immediate alternatives. It seems like he is often cutting off his nose to spite his face, especially in his professional life.

Too many of us are like Jack—we have only one set of patterns and scripts for use on all occasions, a sort of one-size-fits-all approach. Others among us use familiar patterns and habits, sometimes with minor adjustments, in too many situations, regardless of how well they serve us. The fact that we repeat these tapes and behavioral patterns, or their variations, across different situations or aspects of our lives does not mean that they are impossible to change. It simply means that changing or banishing them requires real effort and commitment.

There is one more important thing we bring to work along with our technical and behavioral strengths and weaknesses. That is our expectations, our hopes, and our concerns. Think about the last time you started a new job. Your expectations probably targeted three areas—the new job itself, the organization you were joining, and the people you were going to work with. A lot of things influenced your particular combination of hopeful and worrisome expectations on that occasion—how you felt about the job and the organization, whether you already knew people who worked there, and what you experienced during the interviewing and hiring process. Your own habits and behavior patterns influence your expectations, too. A Martyr, always fearing the worst, no doubt has an excess of worries. When Charles and his colleague established their medical practice twenty years ago, you can imagine how nervous Charles was. Would they get enough patients to support their growing young families and pay back the loans necessary for all the expensive equipment they would need? How many years would it take? What if the two of them did not work together as well as they thought they would? Had they really chosen the best location for their office? A Tap Dancer, unwilling to commit, may try to avoid having any expectations at all. That is why Jack is more comfortable as a freelancer. By avoiding a permanent professional commitment, he also avoids the risk of having his expectations dashed.

Expectations about a brand new job may be very vague, since they are probably based on fairly limited information. As we are in a job longer, two things happen to those initially vague expectations. First, and not surprisingly, they become more specific. But second, and perhaps more dangerously, they are more and more influenced by our own habits. Our bus driver automatically takes them over along with our other behaviors. Of course Elaine expects to work overtime; leaving the office before seven or eight in the evening feels unnatural to her, unless she has a community meeting to attend. And Chip has become resigned to the fact that some of his customers have very unrealistic expectations of what he can do for them and seem to be taking advantage of his "good nature." Whatever they may be, expectations that are part of our self-defeating behavior patterns *will be met.*

What We Find at Work

The first and most significant thing we find is the job itself. We are there to perform the job, and it provides the core of the satisfaction and self-esteem that we need from our work. Some jobs are a lot better than others at providing these intangible benefits. All jobs are much more than their formal job descriptions and more than all of the additional tasks that fall under the notorious phrase "other duties as required." A job also structures our relationships with the people we work with and for—fellow employees, customers/clients, and others—and with the organization as a whole. These two things, the people and the organization, are the two other important things we find when we get to work. And it is these relationships, not the job alone, that are our real interest. The next chapter will be devoted to the people, but first we need to understand more about the organization where we find ourselves.

Systems and How They Operate

We all were born into and live in an array of systems. Some of these systems—work, church, school, some social or recreational groups—are formally structured as organizations. Others, most importantly our families, are not. But they are all systems; whether or not those groups or systems are formally organized, our relationships within them follow similar patterns. For example, like Charles, some of us are always willing to go the extra mile, sacrificing our own needs or desires if necessary. Or like Chip, others of us seem regularly to promise more than we can deliver. In fact, the very regularity of these behavior patterns presents even more questions: How do we get to be really good at solving certain kinds of problems or handling particular types of people or situations? Why don't we cope with certain other types of people, situations, or problems very well? Is there a difference? Can you do something about it?

Because our focus is on the workplace and how we operate there, we need to begin with systems and organizations. A system is a network of interdependent relationships that involves communication, decision making, and action. It has a structure and a function of its own, separate from and greater than the sum of its parts. It is complete within itself. Some systems are fairly simple, such as thermostats or single-celled creatures, while others, manufacturing plants or the human body, are extremely complex. Some, like thermostats, are called *closed systems* because they operate in a single loop, responsive only to internally specified signals or information. That is, only the preset temperatures that automatically turn heating or cooling on or off can control this system.

Families or work groups, the kinds of systems that we are concerned with here, are examples of *open systems*. Open systems are able to accept and respond to a wide variety of new, outside information. They receive all kinds of information from everywhere. That is, they are not confined to receiving only certain kinds of signals from specified sources. They have the ability to change and adapt to new circumstances, in contrast to closed systems, which do not. In fact, in order to function well and remain healthy, open systems need to pay attention to both their internal and external environments. And they need to do more than use new information that comes their way; they actually need to seek it out when it is hidden or elusive.

This capacity to adapt and change is the strength of open systems. Open systems that ignore such information, attempt to avoid change, or pretend that they are closed systems inevitably become dysfunctional. The disintegration of the Soviet Union's control over Eastern Europe and its own internal decay provide a dramatic example of the ultimate futility of such efforts. Systems of any size, from large corporations to families, can become dysfunctional and even disintegrate for the very same reasons. One of the reasons codependency creates such serious problems for both individuals and organizations is the fact that it can, and often does, limit ability to receive and act upon information.

Jack provides a good individual example—his unwillingness or inability to make long-term commitments has prevented him from hearing some important positive feedback and advice on his artistic talent. It has also kept him from considering at least two job offers that could have developed his talent and furthered his career significantly. His professional promise, once glowing, grows dimmer and dimmer. Neglect or suppression of information can also damage organizations. We will have much more to say about that later.

All systems—large or small, simple or complex, open or closed—are internally consistent. All require consistent behavior from their constituent parts, whether those parts are the electronic circuits of a computer chip, the organs of our bodies, or the human members of an organization. In human systems, traditions and norms enforce that consistency by defining expected ways of behaving and relating. In addition, organizations—as complex open systems made up of individual people—have ways of rewarding people for behaving in the appropriate manner and of punishing those who do not.

This internal consistency is true of both formally structured groups like business organizations and those, such as families, that are not. And it is true of systems that are healthy and those that are not, that are dysfunctional. For instance, Charles has carried his sense of responsibility to his colleagues, to the practice, and to their patients to the point where it has certainly become dysfunctional for him, and probably for the practice as well. Though he surely bears a share of the burden for this state of affairs, over the years the other members of the group have done their share as well. Charles has relieved them of some of their legitimate responsibilities by agreeing to substitute or fill in for them. The group as a whole is likely not as strong as it could be if each member was pulling his or her full weight. In turn, they have encouraged and rewarded his behavior by trusting him to care for members of their own families and implicitly acknowledging his primary leadership role. Any change now would obviously jar this particular consistency of their little system seriously.

The Organization as a System

We all, each and every one of us, work in some kind of system. It may be as large and complex as a huge international corporation or as small and simple as the office of your family dentist. All organizations are open systems and, because they are made up of people, they resemble people in some important ways. They are able to accept and respond to new information and able to change. They may be healthy or unhealthy, flexible or rigid, open or closed, stable or erratic. That is, *they may develop some of the same kinds of codependent habits that people have.* But before we get to those dysfunctional organizational patterns, we need to spend some time on what organizations are like and how they function generally. Organizations—like people—have values, norms, and expectations. And they model and reinforce behavior patterns that support those values, norms, and expectations. They also provide a wide array of tangible and intangible benefits.

Large organizations, and even medium-sized ones, also consist of multiple systems and subsystems. These various systems come in three basic types—technical systems, human systems, and sociotechnical systems—plus an array of more specialized subtypes. A manufacturing company, for instance, would have a machinery system, a materials system, and control systems such as accounting and management information. A service organization, such as a social service agency or a hospital, has its service delivery systems and supplies systems as well as control systems. Governments have their executive systems with an array of departments and agencies, legislative systems, and judicial systems.

Technical systems, of course, vary according to the basic nature of the business or organization. All types of businesses and organizations, however, must have human systems to control and operate the others, and most need sociotechnical systems to manage the relationships between the human and technical systems. Then, to top it all off, the human systems have both formal and informal systems. The formal system, of course, is the one published in the official organization chart. The informal one, operating right alongside it, is how the organization really functions and gets its work done. All these systems overlay and interact with each other, multiplying the complexity. It makes you wonder sometimes how anything actually gets done.

Think about your present work system and its characteristics. The two most significant systems in author Earnie's work life could not be more different. The first twelve years of his professional life were spent as a Catholic priest, working with young people in inner cities in the American Midwest. The Roman Catholic Church is as large and complex an international organization as any international business corporation could ever hope to be. Even the local, inner city parishes were fairly complex sets of subsystems with their schedule of formal services, myriad social service activities, schools, and so on.

Although it allows some variety and creativity in its service programs, the Church is rigid in its doctrine and hierarchical structure and in the values and world view it promotes. It models and reinforces and rewards those within the system who exemplify and support those values and norms. The Church is very stable, and changes over the centuries have been at the pace of the tortoise, not the hare. This stability has been an important source of its strength, and of the comfort and security it provides to those within its fold, from priests to parishioners.

Since leaving the church, Earnie's pursuits as counselor, writer, and lecturer led him to start a small business to organize and carry out these activities. Though it sometimes seems too complex and busy for his tastes, this system is tiny and simple by comparison to the Catholic Church. It is open and flexible, able to adapt quickly to the emerging needs of Earnie and his family, a small staff, and—most of all—his clientele. He tries to model and reinforce the values that he stands for—openness, change and growth, and attainment of one's full potential as a healthy, self-enhancing individual.

His present system is certainly more comfortable for him than his last years in the Church. This probably says as much about him as about the Church and is not intended as a putdown of the Church and the many fine things it stands for and accomplishes. Rather, it emphasizes how important it is for all of us to live and work in organizational systems that meet our needs and share our values. It is also important for us to believe that we count for something in our organization, that we can have some influence in the system. It is just as important that everyone work together from shared values and shared respect for each other.

Norms, Values, and Expectations

The sketches of these two contrasting systems are very brief and superficial, but they may give you some clues about the values and norms of your own organizational system and ways to think about them. Values are almost never discussed openly, but they are widely shared throughout the organization and form the basic underpinnings of the system. Does an organization place great stock in its traditions, or is it always looking for new and better ways of doing things? Does it emphasize the profitability above all else or the quality of its products or services? Is it concerned about its place in its community and its contributions to quality of life, or does it see the world as a place where only the fittest and toughest can survive? Does it delegate responsibility to the lowest possible level and encourage risk taking, or will caution and buck passing rule the day? These are just a few examples of the kinds of questions that an examination of values can answer.

Norms emerge from values. Like values, norms themselves are also invisible. They are the organization's habits or behavioral patterns, the drivers of its bus. We do not talk about norms very often, simply because we do not need to. Everyone automatically knows, or learns pretty quickly, what is expected or required—"the way we do things around here." Probably the most typical situation in which norms are openly mentioned is when it is necessary to pull a new employee aside and explain, "You know, Chip, before you promise one of your customers that you will get some new equipment installed and running in record time, you really need to check first with the people in tech support. They work on tight schedules and that one last week really stretched them. You owe them one now."

Organizations have norms about all kinds of behaviors—everything from how to dress appropriately, whether it is okay to eat lunch at your desk, what types of decisions must be passed up to the boss, how customers or clients are treated, or whether it is acceptable to disagree openly in meetings. In other words, an organization's norms become visible in the form of the behavior of the people who work in that organization. In the Walt Disney organization, the strict and detailed dress code norms at Disneyland and Disney World are openly addressed. All potential male employees, for instance, are informed that no facial hair is permitted. That is, beards or mustaches have to go. Period. Only Walt's own pencil-slim mustache survived. In Earnie's organization one of the norms is that members reach decisions by consensus. And they support that norm with another one; it really is okay to express opinions and to disagree. Needless to say, such norms differ from an extremely hierarchical system like the Catholic Church where lots of things are not open for any discussion at all.

Norms and the values that support them join to create expectations—organizational expectations of how we will behave. Just as we bring our own expectations to work with us, when we get there we discover that the system has its own expectations for us. And some of those expectations may be surprises, things we did not know when we signed up. Naturally there is the expectation that we will all do our jobs well. Expectations about job performance are generally fairly clear these days, especially in organizations that have formal appraisal systems, and their number is rapidly growing.

Systems also expect that we will conform to their norms and expectations. So what happens if you don't? The short answer is, "It depends...." It depends on the seriousness of the violation and on the frequency. Enough people violating a particular norm often enough may mean that the norm is changing or disappearing. It also depends on whether the violation seems to be a way of testing the system or a serious challenge to the basic values and practices of the organization. In any case, violators are pressured to conform. But woe unto those who persist in serious challenges. When they finally go too far, churches excommunicate and employers fire.

An important norm or expectation in most organizations is *teamwork*. Of course, a cooperative team spirit is essential to any organization. People need to pull together and help each other out. We need to know that we can count on our co-workers. Chip made a promise to his customer that actually was not his to keep. His co-workers in tech support had to make good on it. He needed their cooperation, but they also needed his. This kind of situation happens all the time, and so do plenty of others requiring cooperation and mutual support.

Healthy and Unhealthy Systems

Organizations do a lot of things *for* us, whether they are healthy or not. Unhealthy organizations can also do a lot of things *to* us, if we let them. First and foremost, organizations provide us with work—one half of a satisfying, self-enhancing mature life. A job that provides a sense of accomplishment and genuine satisfaction is truly a blessing. There is no question that Charles, despite his worries and sacrifices, finds these things in his medical practice. Except for a few independent souls, like writers, most of us need an organization to structure our work lives.

Organizations also provide us with an array of tangible and intangible benefits. The tangible benefits are easy to identify—salary and other benefits such as insurance, retirement, time off, and so on. Besides work satisfaction, the intangibles may include such things as power and prestige, a sense of purpose, and a social network. Healthy or not, all organizations provide the tangible benefits for us.

It is when we get to the intangible benefits that unhealthy organizations start messing up and doing things to us. First, like individuals with self-defeating habits, unhealthy organizations take perfectly good, potentially self-enhancing behaviors—or norms—and carry them to a dysfunctional extreme. And second, if one of the organization's dysfunctional norms happens to mesh neatly with one of yours, chances are your own self-defeating habit will grow even stronger. The organization's bus driver leads a parade, and your bus driver falls right in line. This makes your struggle to kill off that habit and replace it with a healthy new behavior pattern that much harder.

No company is formally in the business of providing a social network for its employees. But it is true that most people look to their workplace as a source of social contacts and perhaps even friends. And many organizations do take pride in the sense of family they cultivate among their employees. They offer an array of "extracurricular" activities, from regular informal Friday afternoon get-togethers to sports teams, summer picnics, holiday parties, and such. So far, so good. But participation can become such a powerful norm that people feel that they have no choice. And in some organizations, they hardly do have much choice if they want to stay and remain effective. These organizations have fallen into the first of those two dysfunctional traps—carrying a healthy behavior pattern to an unhealthy extreme.

The most obvious unhealthy behavior pattern that our work organizations encourage and reinforce, of course, is the workaholic one. Neither Elaine nor her law firm is unique. Japanese lower or middle-level office workers or managers routinely put in twelve- to fifteen-hour days. At the end of what we consider a normal work day, they usually go out for dinner and drink with colleagues and customers. It is really a ritualized pattern for these "salarymen," as they are called. Then, say around ten o'clock at night, they may return to their offices for yet another hour or two at their desks! Add to this a one- or two-hour commute each way, and you have a truly vicious behavior pattern that is worse than unhealthy. Their children hardly know them and, worse yet, this terrible pace is literally killing them. The Japanese even have a word for it—"karoshi," which means died from overwork. Although family members and co-workers can clearly identify karoshi, it is rarely listed as the official cause of death, in order to protect companies from liability. Scary, isn't it, how not just the organizational system, but the entire social system of the country can reinforce and model such self-defeating habits?

Or consider Jan, whose caring for her staff interferes with her productivity. It is not just that she has turned her own staff into her family. During the years before she married, she began to use those other company activities to substitute for the family she had never really had. As she advanced into supervisorial positions, it felt only natural to regard her staff as family and treat them just as she had treated her younger brother and sister. But we are getting ahead of ourselves here. The next chapter is about how people's codependent patterns interact with those of the organization to affect both their work and the organization itself.

Before we are ready to move on, we need to understand a little more about dysfunctional organizations. You might try to fit them into the same six types that we are using to describe codependent individuals, but that can be more confusing than helpful. The problem is that organizations are even more likely than individuals to have bits and pieces of several of those types. Also, different parts of a single large organization may have different kinds of self-defeating patterns. Overall, we believe it is more useful to look at characteristics of unhealthy organizations. And there are four that we think are significant.

1. *Unhealthy organizations are more closed than open.*

   Or at least they spend a lot of energy trying to keep themselves as closed as possible. The purpose of all this effort is control. But the price is always high—limited options, both for employees and for the organization itself; narrow and short-sighted vision; missed opportunities; and meanness of spirit. In the long run, the effort is bound to be futile. Even when a system can maintain tight control internally, its external environment remains forever beyond its reach. When the system proceeds to ignore those external factors that it is unable to control, it puts itself at their mercy. And that mercy is never gentle.

   Meanwhile, life inside the system withers from lack of nourishment from the outside. Excessive loyalty is required in this "us versus them" atmosphere, and open expression of feelings is out of the question. No one dares to point out that the emperor has no clothes, at least no one who wishes to remain.

2. *Unhealthy organizations thrive on denial and collusion.*

   These in turn thrive on indirect and muddled communications and breed dishonesty. For a start, ignoring outside information requires senior managers to conspire to deny its very existence. This habit is a contagious one that expands to include internal information as well. Collusion can be a useful technique for papering over differences to avoid conflict. And sweeping inconvenient or difficult information under the rug is remarkably easy once you get used to it.

Consider the CEO of a large corporation who is married to his wife of many years, the mother of his teenaged children, and who lives part-time with his family, but who also spends a large portion of his time with another woman in her apartment in a different section of the city. The second relationship is no secret, and he often brings that woman to private or unofficial social events. So what business is this of his colleagues and subordinates? There is the awkwardness of not knowing which woman will appear on a social occasion. More important are the difficulty of tracking him down nights or weekends, which is often necessary, and the effects of the personal strain, which are beginning to show in his work. While everyone knows of his dual life, everyone avoids confronting him with the problems it is creating for them and for the company. They simply pretend it is not happening. Worse, no senior executives involved are willing to admit that this habit has infected other areas of their work or to face up to the larger implications for the company.

3. *Unhealthy organizations also thrive on excessive change, crisis management, and confusion.*

You probably all know of systems where people say, "Change is a way of life here." Or you have probably heard people complain that "I can never plan on getting anything done because I seem to spend all my time putting out fires." In these organizations people hardly know what "normal" might be like, let alone how they would function in such rare circumstances. Constant change can be just as dysfunctional as too little change. Lurching along from crisis to crisis is more likely to produce spinning wheels than genuine forward progress. So is a revolving door of bosses and organizational charts. The resulting confusion keeps us from knowing what is really going on. It can be another way of masking the lack of solid productivity and real accomplishment. And it prevents us from taking individual responsibility for our actions and our work.

A small mail-order sporting goods distributor provides a good example of excessive change and the confusion it creates. The owners were always on the lookout for new ventures to add to their existing array of activities, especially when everything was humming along so smoothly that they were bored. On one of those occasions, they spied a smokehouse that was doing poorly and seemed ripe for picking. The business smoked a variety of meats and cheeses and sold them by mail order. "How much difference could there be between a smoked salami and a pair of running shoes?" they asked themselves. And they answered, "Not much. After all, people who run have to eat, don't they? Surely enough of them will like a smoked cheese and salami sandwich to make this a good deal." No doubt you have already guessed the outcome of this sad tale. There is a lot more difference between sporting gear and cheese than they imagined, and a lot of time, energy, and money was diverted from the sporting goods business before they finally gave up on the smokehouse. The distraction and confusion caused by this detour seriously damaged the productivity and morale of their employees, whose skills were in designing, producing, and marketing sporting gear, not delicatessen food. Not surprisingly, it took quite a while to recover from this adventure.

4. *Unhealthy organizations promise more than they can deliver.*

They may not intentionally "overpromise," but that is the result. We are not talking here about extravagant promises of large bonuses or fast-track promotions that may be made during the hiring process, though those promises might alert you to this problem. The concern here is really the more subtle promise. One of those is that "we are one big happy family here." A work system may be like a family system in some ways, but it is not actually a family. And it should not try to be. When it does try, it is likely to be like a dysfunctional family—controlling with rigid rules and norms, denying individuality, limiting opportunities, and papering over disagreement with the illusion of harmony.

Another type of false or excessive promises relates to mission and goals. Social service and nonprofit organizations are typically most vulnerable here. Their lofty ideals and service orientation attract people who share these feelings and want to contribute to society. Unfortunately, these systems sometimes go astray. People who join them out of commitment to doing good become disillusioned if they discover that the unspoken goals are really to enhance the power of the executive director, to provide a sense of self-worth to members of its board of directors, to build political power in the community, to increase the size of the agency by getting more and more funding grants, or to preserve the reputation of the agency.

Unhealthy systems sound like pretty miserable places to work, don't they? And, indeed, they often are. So who in their right mind would choose to stay? They include people whose own self-defeating tapes and habits fit neatly with the un-healthy characteristics and habits of the system, people who are more comfortable in a setting where they do not have to make any real decisions because the right and wrong answers are always obvious, people who need the high level of activity that typically masks the lack of real accomplishment, or people who believe, for whatever reasons, that they really do not have any alternative.

Whatever their own issues may be, all too often these people have their own load of self-defeating habits. Take our friend Chip, for instance. True, his co-worker pulled him aside for advice about clearing his promises with tech services, the people who have to keep Chip's promise. But as usual, there is more to tell. The owner of the business is really pushing expansion, and Chip was not the only new salesperson hired. He is also putting a lot of pressure on the sales staff with really high targets, but has established a generous bonus program for anyone who can manage to meet those new targets. The trouble is that he has not expanded the tech services staff as well. This high-pressure, high-stakes environment fits too well with Chip's own dysfunctional habit of trying to gain approval by overpromising.

Organizational Heaven and Hell

There is an ancient Chinese parable about an old man who knew he would die soon. Before he died, he wanted to know what heaven and hell were like. So he visited a wise man in his village to ask, "Can you tell me what heaven and hell are like?"

The wise man led him out of the village and down a strange path, deep into the countryside. Finally, they came upon a large house with many rooms and went inside. Inside they found lots of people and many enormous tables with an incredible array of food. Then the old man noticed a strange thing. The people, all thin and hungry, were holding chopsticks twelve feet long. They tried to feed themselves, but of course they could not get the food to their mouths with such long chopsticks. "This is surely Hell," said the old man. "Now will you show me heaven?"

The wise man led him out of the house and further on the same path. They reached another house, similar to the first, and again entered. The scene was much the same, much food and many people, again with twelve-foot chopsticks. But this time the people were happy and well fed. The old man could not understand. "These people are happy and well fed, but they, too, have twelve-foot chopsticks. Please explain to me," said the old man.

The wise man responded simply, "In heaven, people feed each other."

Healthy organizations may not be heaven. But healthy organizations do nurture healthy behaviors. Healthy organizations also nourish their people and help them to nourish each other.

4

Codependents at Work: The Six Types in the Workplace

R emember that we defined codependency as a person's own personal, unique set of patterns and habits that sabotage or undermine constructive, satisfying relationships. A codependent relationship is one in which the two parties facilitate and reinforce each other's dysfunctional habits. Those two parties, as we learned in the last chapter, do not have to be two people. They can also be one person plus an organization or system.

You have looked at how you began learning the habits and behavior patterns, both useful and dysfunctional ones, that you bring with you to work. You should also have been looking at the baggage that your co-workers—friends, peers, subordinates, and bosses—bring along with them. What kinds of self-enhancing *and* self-defeating behaviors are you and your colleagues typically using? Where do you see yourself and others interacting in positive and satisfying ways? In what kinds of situations are you feeding each other? And where are people *not* helping each other out? Where are you, or they, reinforcing each other's dysfunctional habits and failing to feed each other?

You have been scrutinizing your workplace, too, the system in which you probably spend more active hours each week than any other. How healthy is that organization? Does it nourish you and help you to feed each other? As for you personally, what kind of fit do you find between your expectations and those of the organization? How well do your tapes play there? Do you have some self-defeating tapes that play only too well?

Please heed an important caution before you get carried away with all of these questions and the new knowledge that can help you answer them. Your purpose in paying attention to your co-workers' behavior patterns is certainly not to diagnose what is wrong with them, let alone inform them of your opinion. It is to understand the patterns of your *own* relationships with them better— to recognize and build on the positive elements of those relationships, to acknowledge any other elements that are dysfunctional, and to sort out how your own self-defeating habits are contributing to the dysfunction so you can take steps to improve things. In fact, this is a good point to remind ourselves that being codependent does not automatically mean being "sick." Yes, it is true that some people's codependency problems can become so severe that they need professional help. But being codependent is not like being pregnant—you *can* be a little bit codependent. And it is possible to change those habits by yourself or with a little help from your friends.

Why Is Workplace Codependency So Important?

In the last chapter we said that companies are not in business to provide for our social life. Nor are they in business to

provide for our mental health or to make us better a
people. Companies should care about codependency because
it has severe negative consequences for organizations just as
it has for people. Those consequences occur regardless of
whether we are talking about a system that is itself codependent or about any system that has codependent people working within it. We can safely assume that any organization has
some codependent employees. Those negative consequences
may begin with things like job satisfaction and employee
morale, but they can rapidly expand to affect productivity and
profits. And remember, job satisfaction and good employee
morale are the "foods" that produce and nourish efficiency,
productivity, and profitability.

Before focusing on the importance of codependence to
organizations and why we should care about it, we need to
remind ourselves that not all organizational problems result
from codependency. From performance to profitability, organizational problems can arise from a number of sources.
For example, an organization may be self-defeating when it
lacks clarity about its goals and mission, when it has failed to
maintain or update its equipment, or when it has a weak
understanding of its customer base or its marketplace. Weak
moral and ethical character will also produce organizational
dysfunction. Questionable ethics may be rooted in codependency, particularly for People-Pleasers whose tendency to
overpromise backs them into a corner. But the scandals of
recent years in the financial industry show that dubious
morals may also result from basic greed. Codependency accounts for enough problems without adding greed to its list!

So how and where does codependence bring negative
consequences to organizations? And what are those consequences? Remember the three basic types of systems in organizations—technical, human, and sociotechnical. Where
codependence makes trouble, of course, is in the people parts

of the overall system, in the human and sociotechnical systems. How it makes trouble is basically by introducing distortions into those systems. These distortions may be introduced by codependent individuals within the system—like Jan who has herself surely introduced distortion into her work unit (and her division as well) with her excessive caretaking of her subordinates. Or the distortions may be those very characteristics of unhealthy systems that we discussed in the last chapter—collusion, confusion, overpromising, attempts to keep the system closed, and so on—that have taken root and flourished within the system itself. In other words, organizations themselves can actually be codependent.

As for the consequences, they affect the organization both indirectly, as they affect those who work there, and directly. Specifically, a codependent person often performs at less than full capacity and is likely to get in the way of co-workers and to hinder their performance, too. Worse yet, a codependent person may encourage these self-defeating habits among co-workers. Unfortunately, Jan is guilty here, too, as her manager and his boss have already observed that her unit is the least efficient in their division. Also, her solicitous habits may well be snaring some of her employees, meshing their codependence with hers—she solves their problems; they *let* her solve their problems. Some even seek her out! It is great that Jan is caring and supportive, but not when that behavior takes precedence over her work obligations or when it takes proper responsibility away from those she is helping.

Overall, whether we are talking about codependent people within a system or a codependent system, the negative consequences of the distortions in the system include inefficiency, decreased energy and commitment, lower quality of organizational work life, greater stress, and lower productivity. It is hardly surprising that declining profitability follows. These potent bottom-line issues can have a real impact on long-term organizational health and survival. They explain why concern about organizational codependency is not merely "organizational social work." Any organization that cares about its profitability must also care about codependency. It is why these organizations need to pay serious attention and act. Their bonus is that when they help themselves, they also help their employees.

Codependency in the Workplace: The Six Types and Their Opposites

We have just summarized the consequences of codependency in the workplace in general terms. Now it is time to explore those effects in greater detail in order to understand more clearly their impact on the system, on those we work with and serve, and on the outcome. To begin, we will revisit our six types to take a closer look at the kinds of problems their typical characteristics create. We will also discover that each has a kind of opposite, a mirror image, or a reflection. Undoubtedly, you will recognize some people you know and work with. No real person is a perfect type—many of us have habits from more than one type—and different people become codependent in different ways. Remember that, like much in life, many of these characteristics are beneficial in moderation. It is carrying them to an extreme that creates problems and defines codependency.

Caretakers

The key issue for Caretakers is control. This desire for control is why they are so eager to solve other people's problems, to tell them how to do their work. In fact, in the workplace, the "caretaking" is much more likely to focus on telling other people how to do their work than on solving their personal problems. The trouble here is not just that they are meddlesome or bossy, though they certainly can be. The real problem at work is that they take, and keep, control—control over other people's work and over their own as well. As a result, they neither delegate well, nor make good team players. Delegation is a crucial skill of great importance to the efficient and productive functioning of any organization. You are probably acquainted with the supervisor who assigns a task but does not hand over the authority necessary to carry it out, then continually peers over your shoulder to make sure you are doing it properly. You begin to wonder why you were given the assignment at all if you are not going to be allowed to do it.

If you are beginning to wonder right now whether these folks were bossy even when they were kids, the answer is "maybe." But more to the point is recalling the critical experiences of childhood that we talked about earlier, specifically positive predictability. Among other things, positive predictability gives order to our lives and makes things reliable. When it is inadequate or missing, when our lives seem chaotic, one possible way to cope is to try to exert control over those crazy, unpredictable events. Children are not too likely to be successful in imposing order on family life, but they may be very successful in learning the habits of control—control over what happens to them and control over those around them. And what they are probably *not* learning in these circumstances are interdependence and cooperation.

By their very nature, systems large or small are interdependent and require a great deal of cooperation and team playing to be productive and profitable. No doubt, you also have encountered the co-worker who is uncooperative, who does not share information needed by others. Their need to maintain control leads Caretakers to attempt to create their own closed systems that minimize the information that both comes in and goes out. They can be enormously proprietary about their work, as if they had put up fences around the borders of their projects with signs warning, "My Project, Keep Out." This degree of control is, of course, impossible. But they do succeed in creating bottlenecks and other inefficiencies, in producing stress, and in reducing productivity.

The situation can be very hard if this kind of Caretaker is the boss or, worse yet, the owner of an international publishing empire like the late Robert Maxwell, former owner of the *Daily News* in New York, MacMillan books in Boston, and an array of other businesses in the United States, London, and elsewhere. By all reports, Mr. Maxwell was an extremely difficult, if talented, man to work for. An article in *The Wall Street Journal* quoted one of his key executives who said, "He's a hard man to live with. He operates as if he is the sun and you are the moon. He loves to do things himself—and more often than not he is right. But the question is, can he do it all in a 24-hour day? Can anyone?" Another executive resigned abruptly after being severely chewed out at a meeting for doing things that Maxwell himself had approved earlier. And the general counsel of one of his companies attributed her resignation in part to the fact that she was never able to obtain even a list of the very companies she was supposed to represent legally.

Who needs to work for anyone as controlling as Maxwell was reputed to be? Evidently not several of the top executives who quit during the last couple of years of his life. In addition, he could be very unpredictable, another trait typical of those who strive to maintain total control. Keep everyone off balance, make sure they will be surprised by what you do next. So he snarled or sunk more than one major deal in which he was either the buyer or the seller. Asked by a reporter whether he was hard to get along with, Maxwell replied, "I get along fine with myself." This may have been fine for him, but it was not so fine for his organization, his business objectives, or those who worked for him—as subsequent disclosures have shown.

We have already met the Caretaker's opposite, the Baby who is all too willing to surrender control and responsibility. When these two are thrown together or find each other, the Caretaker and his/her opposite are likely to unite to form a codependent relationship—a particularly strong one since their codependencies mesh so well. This kind of symbiotic relationship, especially between a boss and key subordinate, will surely magnify the problems either can make for the organization individually. On the surface, Babies may appear to be model employees and subordinates, but they require an inordinate amount of supervision and cannot be counted on to pull their weight. Their passivity and indecisiveness are as damaging to an organization as their Caretakers' over-control, and in much the same way—by creating bottlenecks, inefficiency, and stress.

People-Pleasers

People-Pleasers cannot say "no" because their driving motivation is to avoid conflict. As we have said earlier, they will go to almost any length to achieve this goal. Cooperation is essential to the smooth operation of any system, but it does not require absence of conflict. True cooperation requires coping with conflict in a straightforward and effective way so that it can be resolved constructively. People-Pleasers do not believe that this is possible and have never developed the skills to do so. Instead, convinced that conflict is always destructive, they have become very skillful in avoiding it.

The most obvious explanation for the development of this type of codependence is, of course, growing up in a conflict-filled or even violent environment and learning somehow to avoid rather than join in. This explanation is surely true of some People-Pleasers. Others may have been reinforced early and often for being "good" little boys or girls. They soon learned about the benefits they could reap with their winning ways. The proverbial daughter who can "wrap her daddy around her little finger" probably started honing her People-Pleasing skills while bouncing on his lap. Along the way they may collect sneers for being the "teacher's pet" and, unfortunately, fail to learn that substance often counts for more than style.

People-Pleasers' opposites are Warriors, who are also trapped by emphasis on style of behavior. We call them Warriors because they are adversarial people who actively seek out confrontation and typically see situations in win-lose terms. Since these two types are genuine opposites, their patterns of codependency do not mesh like those of Caretakers and Babies. In fact, they often intentionally avoid each other because their styles are so incompatible. Warriors are the bane of the existence of any genuine People-Pleaser, who will inevitably come out of any tangle with a Warrior the worse for it. As for Warriors, the People-Pleaser's willingness to go to any length to avoid conflict takes away all the challenge and fun.

The failure to manage conflict effectively is the most common problem we encounter in our work both with organizations and with individuals. This is not to say that the world has more People-Pleasers and Warriors than any of the other codependent types. Instead, it shows that all too many of us did not start learning constructive conflict resolution behaviors early enough in our lives. Many of us were learning to avoid conflict and some of us to seek it out. This common learning gap also demonstrates the point that hardly anyone is a perfect example of any of our six types. Because conflict management is such a widespread problem, we will be talking about it in greater length later.

Martyrs

Responsibility is the positive characteristic that Martyrs carry to excess with worry and guilt. Underlying their worry and guilt is a deep-seated fear of success. Where does this overdeveloped sense of responsibility and its companion, success anxiety, come from? How was it learned? Think back to the critical childhood experiences we talked about earlier. One of them was being valued and trusted. When regularly present, this experience produces a sense of achievement. But when it is missing, children are likely to become convinced that something is terribly wrong—that they have done and keep on doing bad things or, more damaging, that they are fundamentally bad people. The end result is worry, guilt, and shame.

Sometimes these feelings begin with small, apparently minor incidents that are not balanced by the necessary positive ones that build a sense of achievement and positive self-esteem. Sometimes they grow from serious and continuing abuse. Or perhaps they emerge from too much responsibility being thrust upon a child, more than a youngster can handle successfully. Charles' case, for example, reflected the last of these scenarios. He was just twelve when his father was killed in a freak accident. Right at the funeral, relatives and friends started telling him, "You're the man of the family now. You will have to take your father's place and take good care of your mother and your two younger sisters." These comments represented an enormous burden for a boy old enough to have some understanding of what that could mean but not yet equipped to measure up to such a challenge. As successful as his professional career has been, Charles remains unable to accept and enjoy it. He continues to seek the success that eluded him as a boy trying to carry out the charge to take his father's place; he continues to worry that he still does not measure up. And he still fears that what he has achieved will all evaporate when people discover that he was not man enough to fill his father's shoes.

So what is the impact of this baggage that Charles and other Martyrs bring to work with them? Unlike Caretakers who smother other people with their controlling ways, Martyrs smother themselves with their own worry and guilt. Always focused on the downside risks, they stifle their initiative and creativity. They fail to see opportunities or, seeing them, fail to seize them and follow through. If only they were not such wet blankets and allowed themselves more creativity, they could function as "devil's advocates." But their typical pessimistic view of everything usually robs them of the credibility necessary to fill this role effectively.

Martyrs also block the free flow of information, but, again unlike Caretakers, they do so for different reasons. When something goes amiss, their approach is not to share the problem but to try to solve it themselves. "Don't worry," they will say, "I'll take care of it" — even when they cannot or should not because the problem is not theirs to solve or because they will not choose the most efficient or creative solution.

The Martyr's fear of success is mirrored in the Procrastinator, who fears failure and criticism. Everyone puts off unpleasant or unwanted tasks from time to time, but the true Procrastinator presents a genuinely self-defeating behavior pattern. Routine assignments may be completed with reasonable competence and efficiency. It is the unusual task or challenging assignment that presents problems, for these present the Procrastinator with the possibility of criticism or failure. Better to avoid, to delay, to be busy with something else, or — as a last resort — to pretend to be working on it. Anything to avoid the worst, but all-too-likely disapproving, outcome. We hardly need add that these folks do not contribute to productivity or profitability. In fact, they directly detract from them.

Perfectionists

Perfectionists suffer from similar problems of low self-esteem as Martyrs do, but they try to resolve them in a different way. Rather than worrying and trying to do too much, they strive never to make a mistake, and they typically expect the same standard of performance from those they work with. Like all the types of codependents, most Perfectionists begin learning this behavior pattern in childhood. No doubt some have modeled a perfectionist parent—the kind who looked at a report card with several A's and a single B and failed to acknowledge the A's, saying only, "Well, we'll certainly have to do something about that B, won't we." Others might be youngsters who tried as hard as they could whenever they could to win approval and acceptance. Unlike those who were burdened by too much responsibility too soon, these kids felt undervalued. Since praise was rarely, if ever, forthcoming, no matter how hard they tried, they concluded something must be really wrong with them. Regardless of the origins, adult Perfectionists are still trying to bolster their self-esteem by avoiding all errors and banishing all defects; they are still afraid that mistakes will reveal that they are basically flawed.

In their devotion to quality and excellence, Perfectionists go beyond encouragement to "be the best that you can be" or beyond reasonable requirements for quality products, services, and job performance. The trouble, of course, is that their standards are unattainable, by themselves or by others. And they have become unable to acknowledge two things. First, those standards are indeed unrealistic. Second, they have distorted their commitment to excellence by developing the habit of using perfection to enhance their frail self-image. In contrast to Procrastinators, who often become paralyzed by their need to avoid criticism or failure, Perfectionists simply strive all the harder to reach their elusive goal.

One of the difficulties in dealing with perfectionism as a problem is that its basic aim, the pursuit of excellence, is both necessary and admirable. Every organization must perform well and produce high-quality goods or services if it is to survive in the long-run, and many corporations have sizeable quality control staffs. It is, as usual, by carrying a good thing too far that Perfectionists become self-defeating, both for themselves and their organizations. Their obsession with perfection often slows down the flow of work, as they make one more computer run, review things yet again for any errors, and so on. Also, they are often unwilling to recognize different levels of importance, to distinguish between those tasks or projects where precision and perfection are critical and others where different priorities, such as turnaround time, take precedence. These people assert that anything worth doing is worth doing well—no matter how long it takes. A rough draft, for example, makes sense when several people need to review and contribute to the final written product. Or a message to a long-standing colleague may be brief and to the point, where the same message to a stranger might well need to be longer and more formal.

The son of a friend provides a good example of a Perfectionist in two different types of jobs. Michael grew up wanting to be a scientist. When he completed his graduate degree, he was snapped up by a rapidly growing new biotech firm. For several years he was happy in his laboratory. The work went slowly as basic science often does. And, since Michael is a perfectionist, his work went even more slowly as he painstakingly repeated experiments to reverify the results and as he readjusted his computer models over and over to make sure he was headed in the right direction. Finally it all paid off with a major breakthrough that led rather quickly to an exciting new product.

So far, so good. But recently Michael called to talk about a problem. He was promoted out of the laboratory to the position of product manager for his creation. The problem was the new job. Not only did he miss his lab, but he really did not understand how to work with all these new kinds of people. There were so many demands for things that should have been done yesterday, people needing problems solved right now, staff members reporting to him whose work he did not really understand well enough to feel comfortable. His typical working style—careful, methodical, independent, thoughtful—did not suit his new circumstances. He had been told that his subordinates said he was driving them crazy with his demanding standards, and one of them actually quit after less than a month on his team.

This story does not have an ending, at least not yet. It was pretty easy to figure out what was happening, to start to talk with him about the nature of the problem and about how to help him, and what that will mean for him. But it is not going to be very easy for him to do what he needs to do for himself and to cope with his new job simultaneously.

Perfectionists' opposites are not slobs, for no enterprise can tolerate sloppiness. Perfectionists, who accord full and identical importance to all tasks, are mirrored by laid-back Pollyannas, who also fail to distinguish among their tasks. But Pollyannas approach them all equally casually. While everything is important to Perfectionists, Pollyannas deny importance to almost everything. It is often hard to get them to focus, to pay attention, to set priorities, or to live with priorities that others set for them. And these traits are magnified when Pollyannas must confront problems. If it is hard to keep them on track when things are going smoothly, it is nearly impossible to force these eternal optimists to focus on problems and buckle down to devising and implementing solutions.

Pollyannas do not create the kind of stress among co-workers and subordinates that Perfectionists are capable of; in fact, they can be a lot more fun. They have learned too well that the world is very safe for play, and they do not seem to know how to separate the significant from the trivial. Perhaps like their opposites, the Perfectionists, they were not adequately valued and trusted as children. But they went in the opposite direction, becoming too nonchalant rather than too serious. As a result, they often fail to carry their load and are certainly not great contributors to productivity and profitability.

Workaholics

The label Workaholic has become so common in our language and life, and its issues so self-evident, that there would seem to be little need to discuss this type. How Workaholics' behavior becomes self-defeating for themselves is assumed to be well known. But it does seem odd to think of it as harmful to the workplace. Closer examination of both these issues will reveal otherwise.

Some of the standard assumptions about Workaholics are generally true—they work extremely long hours, often at risk to their health and always to the detriment of their family and social relationships. Other common assumptions are not necessarily true—first, that they are unusually productive and successful in their chosen work; second, that their hard work serves either the goal of providing security for their families or of attaining personal career ambition, or both. Some are productive high-achievers, to be sure, but not all Workaholics are. Here we begin to encounter the downside, the codependency of genuine Workaholics. Many Workaholics, as we pointed out earlier, live their lives in a never-ending pattern of "busyness." Yet their accomplishments never seem to match their level of activity. You begin to get the idea that their objective is activity for its own sake. Especially when you start noticing that these folks never relax, that the busyness pervades all parts of their lives, not just their work lives.

The second doubtful assumption opens the question of motivation—why do people develop these habits? Why do they become Workaholics? And the answer to these questions is not that they are driven by need for security for themselves and their families, for fame and fortune and power, or for service to others. Rather, it is that they have learned to feel worthwhile only when they are working. This is the difference between Workaholics and others who work hard and put in long hours. Workaholics have learned to base their self-esteem on working, on being always busy. Thus, some Workaholics do not spend excessively long hours at their jobs. They work shorter hours because they have plenty to do elsewhere—projects at home, community activities, sports, and so on. Things that others do for fun and relaxation, Workaholics often manage to turn into work.

How did they come to misplace so much emphasis on activity at the expense of accomplishment, fun, and those they care about? If their motivations are not those we tend to assume, what are they trying to cover up or avoid? What Workaholics are generally attempting to hide from is their fear of intimacy and, as a result, their basic loneliness. They may have started learning the pattern from a Workaholic parent, like Earnie did. Earnie's father taught all of his kids that they had to work harder than anyone else. If the job starts at 8:00, be there at 7:30. By the time Earnie was seven years old, he knew that "Larsens work hard!"

The very parents who modeled hard work may also have accounted for the beginning of the loneliness. Those parents forgot—or never understood—that the true "work" of childhood is play. They were so busy teaching their children how to work, they failed to encourage and allow them to play. At the very least, such parents instill the notion that play is unproductive and a waste of time; at worst, that play is a wicked temptation, the devil's work for idle hands. Whichever, those children learn that the world is not safe for play and, in the long run, miss out on the bonds of friendship and intimacy they need to be learning to form. Finally, isolation and chronic loneliness breed a fear of intimacy. Because it has been unknown, intimacy has become strange and uncomfortable, something to be avoided.

Intimacy is not required in the workplace, it is true. Sometimes, in fact, it is best avoided there. So whatever can be the workplace problems created by these apparently hardworking people? The problem is that keeping busy is often the enemy of working smart. Keeping busy can mean lengthening the task, adding "make work" if necessary, to remain occupied. It can mean an inability to say "no." Workaholics, of course, avoid saying "no" for different reasons than other codependent types do. They avoid it because they do not want to pass up an opportunity for more activity, no matter whether the task is suitable for them or for their job. Failure to prioritize also often accompanies this need to stay busy. As work piles up, assignments are pursued in a hodgepodge fashion with too many in various stages of completion. And probably too many are overdue, but how would one know for sure? In other words, bottlenecks, inefficiency, and low productivity all too often characterize the work patterns of Workaholics.

Tap Dancers

Workaholics are not mirrored by a new type about to be introduced. They find their reflection in the last of our basic six types, the Tap Dancer—and vice versa. Where Workaholics fear intimacy, Tap Dancers fear rejection. Where Workaholics overcommit themselves to hide their loneliness, Tap Dancers avoid commitment to hide their self-doubt and lack of confidence. Workaholics are usually around, keeping their typical long hours, and are usually reliable about completing their assignments. Tap Dancers are not necessarily unreliable, but their attention is at least as much on the future, or somewhere else, as on the here and now.

Superficially, Tap Dancers often seem to resemble Pollyannas with their casual, breezy ways, but underneath they really do take things seriously. They take the matter of commitments—professional or personal—so seriously that they go to a lot of trouble when necessary to evade them. If other people really do not get to know them, if they do not become involved in long-term relationships, they will disappoint neither others nor themselves. And they will not be rejected.

Where did this fear come from? Recall Freud's insistence on the equal importance of work and love in the lives of mature adults, then wonder, "Why are Tap Dancers willing to stunt both areas of their lives?" Most likely, they were rejected or abandoned as children, or *felt* that they were even if that did not happen literally. Whatever their histories, they missed those critical experiences that would have generated confidence in long-run commitments. Sadly, they did not learn to trust. They did learn to dodge commitments.

Our friend Jack was certainly not rejected as a child. Or certainly it would not seem so. If anything, he appeared to be an overindulged son of well-to-do parents. It is true that both of them held important and demanding positions that required a lot of work and frequent travel. But they always had a live-in housekeeper, sent Jack to fine schools and excellent summer camps, made sure he had a generous array of educational and fun toys, and sometimes were able to take him along on their foreign travels. In short, they made sure that he had all the privileges neither of them had as children. The problem, of course, was that Jack never actually had either of them as parents. He seemed like just another piece in the complex jigsaw puzzle of their lives, no more important than most of the other pieces.

The unsettled feeling that grew in Jack as he grew up became permanent somewhere along the way. One result for him, as for many Tap Dancers, is that he has never fulfilled his early promise, the potential of his talent. Once again, we encounter the mirroring of Workaholics and Tap Dancers. Just as concern over fear of intimacy is not a priority for employers, why should they be concerned about Tap Dancers' lack of self-confidence and fear of rejection? There is a good reason why they should. In these times of economic dislocation and fierce domestic and international competition, employers do need to be concerned with maximizing the potential of their employees in order to maximize the potential of their businesses. People like Jack are unable to commit, either to themselves— their own skills, talents, and careers— or to their employers. The result is not only a loss of talent, but also a loss of productivity. And these losses— to our society as a whole as well as to individual employers— are losses that we can all ill afford.

The effects of each of the six types of codependents' behaviors give us a solid start on the problems codependency creates in the workplace. But understanding these behavioral effects is just a start. In the next chapter we will continue to explore the havoc it produces by looking at organizational or systemic issues. And later, we will look at the options available to those of us who are not codependent, but who find ourselves working with others who are or with codependent systems.

5

Workplace Issues

We focused on the six codependent types to examine the problems each of them create in the workplace—how their habits damage efficiency, productivity, and harmony. Did you just say, "Wait a minute! I understand 'efficiency' and 'productivity,' but what do you mean by 'harmony'? Where did that come from?" What we mean by "harmony" is freedom from hassle and reduction of stress—in other words, quality of work life.

We believe that these three elements are the keys to the bottom line of every organization and that harmony is just as important to that outcome as the other two. While profitability is the standard measure for private organizations, we must not forget that maximizing value for resources used is just as important for public and nonprofit organizations. After all, as taxpayers and contributors we all share in providing their financial resources. So for all organizations—private, public, or nonprofit—that "bottom line" consists of fulfilling their basic purposes and carrying out their missions in an efficient, productive, and harmonious fashion.

As we saw in the last chapter, codependency affects all three of these key elements. Negatively. Now we are going to explore these workplace problems from a different point of view. Instead of looking at the people themselves, we will look at the codependency issues, those problems that must be faced in order to do something about that bottom line. Shifting from a person-centered to a problem-centered viewpoint is useful because it provides us with a new cut on the dilemmas of codependency. But more important, it will direct us toward solutions suitable for the workplace. These will be solutions that target the trio of key bottom line elements—efficiency, productivity, and harmony.

Common Themes Among the Six Types

As we delved into the six types of codependents in the last chapter, you probably noticed some common themes. Several problems are typical of more than one type. Although they may occur for different reasons, the organizational consequences are the same no matter which type is creating the problem or why. So now we are going to talk about codependents in general and the difficulties they have in four critical areas:

- managing conflict
- communicating and sharing information
- working smart
- building and maintaining relationships

Again, in these four areas, a common theme will emerge. It is, in our view, the bottom line of codependency— codependency sets limits. It narrows vision. It restricts possibilities. *It cramps one's style!* Linda Moore, a colleague who has also worked with codependents for many years, describes this basic consequence of codependency with a wonderful metaphor from childhood. Remember coloring books and the process of learning to color? And remember what you were taught was the best, the ideal coloring? Codependency is that ideal—coloring perfectly, inside the lines.

From a systems or organizational point of view, there are times when following a preset pattern carefully and completely is just fine. Take a bookkeeper, for example, or an engine mechanic. We really do not want people in these kinds of jobs being too creative. This approach usually works well when problems are simple and the environment stable, when tried and true solutions are called for. But when initiative, imagination, or creativity are required, the limitations codependency imposes quickly become obvious. The Chinese have a traditional curse—"May you live in interesting times." We surely are living in interesting times. Consequently, codependency, with its narrow constraints and tight boundaries, is truly a curse. It is a personal curse on those who suffer its pain, and it is a curse on organizations trapped in its tentacles.

Managing Conflict

Nothing demonstrates more clearly the limitations that codependency imposes than the widespread difficulties so many people have in their efforts to manage conflict. And no one demonstrates those difficulties more clearly than People-Pleasers, fellows like Tom, who was a member of a codependency support group Earnie once led. You might call Tom a freelance entrepreneur, a venture capitalist who parlayed savings of a few thousand dollars into a net worth of several million in a dozen years. In Tom's view, the key to his success was acceptance of him as a person, by the world in general and his colleagues in particular. That acceptance, in his view, required avoidance of any conflict. As we sorted out where this view and behavior pattern came from, he explained that by the time he was five years old, both his parents had become alcoholics. When his mother died soon after his fifteenth birthday, he felt more relief than sorrow and more than a little guilty. Along the way, during those dismal years, like many children of alcoholics, he became very independent for a kid his age. And he learned two additional essentials for success, work hard and keep your nose clean or avoid fights.

When Tom joined our group, his success seemed to be unraveling. He was not broke, but he had lost a couple million dollars in bad deals. Afraid of looking bad, he went ahead with one deal even though he knew that he was listening to the wrong people and that it would not work out. He was beginning to sense that he was about to make the same mistakes all over again. Not only was he wanting, as usual, to be accepted, but this time he sought it from an unreliable crowd. Tom's breakthrough came when he figured out who was driving his bus. It was the five-year-old boy who was still trying vainly to impress the parents who paid more attention to their booze than to him; he was still trying to win their acceptance and approval. Letting those old habits go and replacing them with new ones has not been easy, but Tom began to see the change in himself. What a difference it made, and the changes occurred sooner than he expected! Most important for him, he was no longer making so many problems for himself. And he was learning how to identify these self-defeating behaviors in others as well and how to avoid them.

As mentioned earlier, failure to manage conflict effectively is the most common problem we encounter in working with individuals and organizations. That is why we believe that it is not the private property of People-Pleasers like Tom. It is a much more widespread behavioral habit that keeps turning up in all kinds of people and places. What both individuals and organizations generally do when conflict rears its ugly head is hope that, if ignored, it will disappear. If it refuses to go away, they attempt to patch up its nicks and scratches with a couple of judiciously placed bandages, or they try to sweep it under the rug. If it bursts out from under that hiding place, they circle back to the first option and simply pretend that it is not happening. In addition to denial, collusion is also involved in these inadequate attempts to manage conflict. Just imagine several people standing around the edges of that rug trying to keep the conflict hidden underneath. Well, we all know only too well how successful these evasions usually are.

It is puzzling why so many people seem to be so afraid of conflict. Why do we put so much energy into those evasive actions that rarely work? Why do we fail to confront conflict when it begins, when it is easier to subdue? Why do we let it fester and harden into a mass of unyielding feelings and spread its poison? As youngsters we probably started learning to fear those feelings. Because they are so uncomfortable, even scary sometimes, many of us never learned how to cope with them effectively. Young children, for instance, overhearing fights between their parents, feel impotent and fear that they are the cause. When parents separate or divorce, even older children are anxious and worry, "Who will take care of me?"

Actually, it hardly matters whether we are afraid of the feelings and avoid conflict *because* we have not learned the skills to handle them. It doesn't matter that we have never learned those skills because the feelings are so uncomfortable that we focus on avoiding and evading them. It matters little because the immediate outcome remains the same—lack of skills and avoidance of important issues. The long-term outcome for most people is, if anything, worse. The continual avoidance of conflict issues—sitting on feelings, pretending that those issues and feelings do not exist—sets limits and chokes off possibilities. For all practical purposes, these constraints put a whole range of possible actions and reactions out of bounds. The evasion and pretense consume a lot of energy that could be put to much more constructive purposes. Tom could not say "no" to that new crowd whose approval he was automatically seeking. He could not even allow himself to recognize his distrust of their proposals or to respond to the warnings of his own instincts. As a result, his five-year-old bus driver cost him more than a million dollars.

Tom offers a good lesson in how conflict avoidance can damage productivity, increase stress, and drop straight to the bottom line for a single person. Does the same thing happen in organizations? You bet it does! What else could you expect, even in systems that function effectively, given our premise that most people do not have good conflict management skills? In self-defeating organizations, individuals' lack of competent behaviors joins the same defect in the system itself to reach an obvious outcome—the negative effects multiply.

Two of the four characteristics of unhealthy organizations that we discussed earlier bear directly on conflict management. First, you will remember that those systems try to keep themselves as closed as possible, usually in order to maintain tight control. Invariably, conflict is one of the things to be controlled. And in this context "controlled" does not mean "managed." It means "stifled," no matter what the cost. Second, unhealthy systems thrive on denial and collusion. These habits, denial and collusion, tell us exactly how those systems deal with conflict. They tell us that conflict has not surfaced and been confronted constructively. Instead, it is stifled, hidden, swept under the carpet. And obviously, these controlling, hiding, and stifling behaviors limit options and close out possibilities. These behaviors also increase costs, both the direct costs of doing business and the indirect costs— more stress, less harmony—paid by the people involved.

Frank was another member of the same support group that Tom joined. Frank owns a business, a small manufacturing company, jointly with a colleague. It has been profitable though, frankly, I do not know much about how healthy the system itself is. What I do know is that Frank brought a serious problem to the group—he *"hated* conflict"—and that story illustrates both the direct and the indirect costs of his own self-defeating behavior on his employees and his business.

Since his business has consistently made a profit, Frank really did not want to see how his dysfunctional habits affected the company. But once he finally was able to admit that his behavior was at the root of some of his business problems, he began to recall one example after another. For one thing, he was unwilling to let incompetent people go or even to confront them. "You know, poor Joe has a sick wife. I just couldn't do it." When one of his subordinates, who was also a good friend, had an idea for a new product, Frank had a gut feeling that it would never fly. Frank himself estimates that his unwillingness to confront his subordinate/friend cost the company $40,000 before it finally cut its losses and abandoned the project. And this experience has taught him another lesson about the costs of conflict avoidance—it leads both to poor product development and to poor people or human resources development.

When a conflict situation would finally reach the point where it had to be dealt with, Frank did so by handing it off to a subordinate. As the boss, he reasoned, wasn't he the quarterback, organizing the strategy and calling the plays? Guards and tackles were there for the tough, nasty jobs, weren't they? Eventually he was able to recognize that his analogy was faulty and that the two main consequences of this particular behavior were not what he intended at all. First, it created resentment in the person he stuck with the dirty work; and second, it hindered that person's job performance.

Frank has come to understand that his avoidance of conflict goes back to his relationship with his father, who was a rough, mean man. Actually, that relationship was not what you would call a relationship at all. It consisted mainly of Frank's avoiding his father for fear of being whipped for any misbehavior or disagreement, real or imagined. As you would expect, Frank never learned that there is any such thing as an honest difference of opinion, that confrontation could be anything but violent, that there are other ways of resolving conflict. He still has to affirm regularly to himself, "Conflict is okay!" but he is replacing old self-defeating patterns with new self-enhancing ones. The most exciting thing to me is what he now finds most exciting—the changes he sees around him at work. First and foremost, he has reported, people are so much happier. And this is not just his own subjective opinion speaking. The company has increased the retention rate of its sales and marketing staff to an unheard of 90 percent, in an industry where 40 percent retention is typical. This shows substantial increase in productivity and harmony with a real impact on the net results!

Communicating and Sharing Information

Simply glancing at a few training catalogues and brochures, either internal course offerings by large organizations with active training departments or materials and courses available to the general public, tells us that a great many people must need to improve their communication skills. There are probably more books, courses, self-help materials, and so on available in this broad area than any other. This is surely a measure of how common communications problems are in organizations. Perhaps it is also one more indication of how many people are trapped in codependency.

For various reasons, most codependents are reluctant to share valid information. Caretakers want to control it; People-Pleasers want to recast it in the most positive light; Martyrs want to suffer through by dealing with the situation alone;

Perfectionists, of course, want it to be perfect; Workaholics want to hang on to it for use in their myriad projects; and Tap Dancers want to ignore it. Then, on top of blocking the free flow of information through their organizations, many codependents have poor communication skills.

Open systems live or die by information, or the lack of it, and their mechanisms for sharing it. In our information-dependent culture, convoluted transmission patterns and distorted communications are bound to have an impact on efficiency, productivity, and harmony. Earnie calls this whole huge problem "communications constipation."

Warren heads an important division of a high-tech engineering firm. He is extremely controlling, but whether that behavior is based in codependency or some other kinds of behavioral habits is hard to say. It is obvious that, through his own behavior, he has created a codependent organization. That organization is characterized by denial and collusion and by confusion and crisis management, two of our signs of unhealthy systems. A couple of instances will give you an idea of what goes on there. They are not isolated examples.

First, a short one centers on the accounting department. As the de facto accounting supervisor, Warren reviews all expense vouchers and circles the amount to be paid. And, indeed, the check is always cut for that amount—even when Accounts Payable knows that he has circled the wrong number, or when they know that an overpayment will result because part of the total has already been paid. They have long since learned that it is easier on them to keep track of his errors and answer questions from puzzled payees than to deal with Warren's discovery that they have corrected his mistakes.

You might chalk up Warren's accounting behavior as an idiosyncracy that is a nuisance, but not seriously damaging to the business and its bottom line. Another example did prove to be genuinely damaging, and, unfortunately, it is all too typical of his style. That time he announced to one and all that he would be unavailable for several days. During that brief period, one of his direct subordinates tried desperately and repeatedly to reach him regarding a major engineering facility that suddenly became available for purchase from a competitor. It could have filled an important strategic gap in the business had they moved quickly, but the opportunity was lost—and lost to a much larger and more powerful multinational corporation. The successful buyer leaped at the chance to expand operations into an area that was new for it, though closely related to another longstanding and successful line of business. The upshot, of course, is that Warren's division suddenly had a powerful new competitor.

Not surprisingly, Warren was furious when he found out, and he raked the subordinate over the coals. But the most amazing fact in this tale is that Warren was in his office the entire time! He simply did not want to be bothered. As you are probably figuring out by now, whatever Warren wants, Warren gets. The trouble is, what Warren seems to want— what his *behavior* tells his subordinates that he wants—is total control. He wants it even at the expense of profitability of the business and of the productivity, well-being, and commitment of his employees.

Think for a minute about the effects of behavior like Warren's on those who work for him. By demanding that the accounting staff do exactly what he has indicated on the vouchers, even when they must intentionally be wrong, he has usurped their professional skills. He has disempowered and demoralized them. By manipulating communications and the flow of information between himself and those who work for him, he has in fact done two things. First, Warren may say that subordinates should have done whatever they had to do to get Warren's attention about the facility purchase. But they had all learned long since that he would thwart any attempt to disobey a clear directive and make mincemeat of them. His staff has been so beat up by him so many times in the past that they have given up trying anything that even hints at initiative or independent action.

Second, they spend at least half their time trying to figure out how to deal with him. By refusing communication on any but his own eccentric terms, he has forced them all—and the system itself—into collusion. He has also forced his staff into exhaustion, as they work very long hours in order to both do their jobs and cope with him. Disempowered and pushed into collusion, their individual and collective self-esteem has simply been worn down to its nub. It is no wonder that, in addition to the people in this system, the efficiency, productivity, and harmony are suffering. The real wonder is how long Warren will continue to get away with this sort of behavior, how long until communications constipation shuts the system down.

Working Smart

"Working smart" is one of those phrases that has become a popular buzzword. Originally it probably referred to taking advantage of new technology to become more efficient and productive, making work easier in the bargain. Now, working smart means more than people using technical systems and resources more effectively, enhancing socio-technical systems. It also means improving our use of people resources, the human systems. The bottom line of working smart is focus—focusing your time, energy, and resources. Many codependents are simply not very good at this.

Hoarding information and blocking its free flow through a system—what we were just talking about—is but one example of failing to work smart. Many codependents also commonly indulge in other self-defeating behaviors of this sort, especially when it comes to the human resources and systems.

Examples include not setting priorities in their work, not putting their own skills and talents (or those of others) to good use, or not saying "no" when they should. As a result, they hamper their own efficiency and productivity and that of others. And they leave a trail of disharmony behind them. Their colleagues cannot be certain when their part of a shared project might be ready. Though they may claim to work best under pressure, their bosses cannot count on them to meet deadlines. And their subordinates never know when to expect a new assignment as a result of their inability or unwillingness to plan, to prioritize, or to say "no."

A friend of mine in the catering and restaurant business illustrates the pitfalls of lack of focus and failure to work smart, and an unhappy tale it is. Ellen eased into a business in a way that looked like she was working smart, and at first she really was. A bright person and a quick study, as well as a good cook, she sought good advice on starting a small business. And she followed it. She began on a small scale and built a solid reputation among a steadily growing clientele. In what seemed like no time at all, she added an upscale carry-out to her catering business and soon after found a location for a small cafe.

Ellen's timing was good. An expanding economy supported her growing business. But when the economy shifted into neutral, then reverse, her self-defeating habits overwhelmed her earlier success. She is one of those combination types, both a People-Pleaser and a Workaholic. In good times, her desire to please her customers and her willingness to work hard had served her well. When the economy went into a tailspin—and you know that caterers and restaurateurs are hit hard and early in such times—her need for approval led her to promise more than she could deliver, even given her workaholic habits.

Of course, the combination of the two types compounded her inability to say "no." And on top of being overburdened, like so many Workaholics, she was very disorganized and was unable to set priorities. As her business expanded, she began to keep an office of sorts at both the restaurant and the catering/carry-out locations, but still did a lot of paperwork at home. As a result it seemed that nothing was ever where she needed it, and things began to fall through the cracks. Ellen even hired one of those professional organizers to help her straighten out her offices and plan her time better, but it was too late. As business fell off, she waited too long to let some of her staff go, in her desire to avoid conflict. When she finally realized that she would have to close the restaurant, again it was too little and too late. Her bills had gotten completely out of hand and she lost the remainder of her business as well.

As they say, hindsight is always twenty-twenty. And I must admit that I did not see how bad things had gotten for Ellen or realize until recently how codependent she is. Fortunately, not all stories are as dramatic as hers, but she surely is a classic example of how dysfunctional codependency can be when the going gets tough. In the beginning, things were going well—both things she could control as she was growing her business and things like the economy, which she could not. Her own talents, which are considerable in many areas, served her well, as did the good advice that she sought and used. She could color inside the lines very well. But later, when the things she had no power over deteriorated, Ellen lost control of those things that she might have been able to manage with more self-enhancing behavior. She was unable to revise her vision or to see new alternatives, different possibilities, or solutions to her problems. When a changing environment called for coloring outside the lines, Ellen simply could not do it.

There is another lesson in Ellen's story. It applies to all of us, whether we are in a small and entrepreneurial business like hers, a large bureaucratic corporation, or something in between. Working smart is advantageous under any circumstances, but it becomes vital when the going gets tough, especially in times of crisis. These are the circumstances where failure to work smart leads us into a black hole of confusion, chronic crisis management, and excessive change—another of our characteristics of unhealthy organizations. And this is when codependency shows its true self-defeating colors.

Building and Maintaining Relationships

Codependency affects each and every one of us. Throughout our lives even those of us who are not codependent inevitably encounter others who are. They are people we work, live, and play with. Of course our expectations for the relationships we have at work are different from those in other areas of our lives, and we place different requirements on them. But everyone must deal with workplace relationships, for no one works in a vacuum.

Each of the three kinds of problems we have just been talking about—managing conflict, communicating and sharing information, and working smart—affects the quality of our relationships with our co-workers. At the bottom of most of those problems are the fundamental relationship issues—of intimacy and commitment. And the truth is that, across the board, codependents have a lot of trouble with these issues—managing them, modulating them, or keeping them at levels appropriate to particular relationships. Some, especially Tap Dancers, have trouble with them period.

If you find it unsettling to apply the words "intimacy" and "commitment" to work relationships, think for a minute about what they mean to you. To me, intimacy means openness and a willingness to share, to both give and receive from others.

Commitment is demonstrated by dependability and reliability, a sense of obligation and accountability. Neither is necessarily all or nothing. Both are a matter of degree, and this is where codependents run into trouble. Even when their heads know that, they have not learned the necessary appropriate behaviors. Or they have not learned how to adjust their behavior to fit the different expectations and requirements of various situations. Just as the levels of intimacy and commitment differ among family members or between casual friends, so do they differ from those suitable for the workplace. Still and all, they are as necessary to our working relationships as they are to our personal ones.

Why are intimacy and commitment so important, particularly in the workplace? And why are they so troublesome for codependents? The short answer to the first question is that they are the foundation on which relationships are built and the cement that holds them together and maintains them. We have talked about the importance of teamwork and cooperation earlier, so we hardly need to add that intimacy and commitment are essential to them. Cooperation and teamwork require enough openness and sharing to nurture mutual confidence—confidence that co-workers will share the work load fairly, that they will carry out their responsibilities reliably, that each is accountable to the others and to their product. They require that those working together not only give *to* each other, but that they also are able to receive *from* each other. Those kinds of self-enhancing behaviors produce the harmony so necessary to the bottom line. They are also the kinds of behaviors that codependents, trapped in their self-defeating behavioral habits, have never learned.

Now to the second question—Why do people who are codependent have such a hard time with the intimacy and commitment needed for productive and satisfying relationships? Once more, we must return to those critical experiences of childhood, at least for most people. Again, a story will help us with the answer. Andy is another member of one of my support groups. In partnership with a couple of others, he owns a chain of nurseries. He and another are the horticulturalist and landscaper, while the third member of their trio has the business expertise. Andy has always been rather a loner, a lot better with plants than with people. That set of habits began when he was only five, when his father had a breakdown. After a year or so, his father was able to return to work, but the family's life was never really like it had been before. Though his mother did her best, Andy's confidence in lasting and secure commitments was damaged beyond repair.

What Andy learned from this central event of his childhood was the importance of total self-reliance. Dependence became a "no-no" for him, and "do it yourself" was his unspoken motto. What Andy did not learn as he was growing up was how to respond to intimacy and closeness, how to share and give of himself, and how to receive from others—in other words, how to trust. Now, as an adult, he envies the easy comradery of his other partners, but he does not know how to join in. They certainly value his expertise and seem to value him as a person as well, but they do not really know how to talk with him, nor he with them. Andy is also aware that he is very distant from his employees. For example, he cannot praise a job well done, fearing that even that kind of compliment would open the door to intimacy. He is now starting to learn to share both with his partners and his employees, but it is a difficult change for him to make.

The Critical Experiences—For Adults

Andy, of course, is by no means the only one of our players who has carried into his adult life the effects of missing or damaged critical experiences as a child. So let's take this opportunity for a brief look at how the presence or absence of those experiences in childhood translate from childhood into adulthood. Here are the five critical experiences, again organized in a chart showing how their presence or absence plays out in our work lives:

CRITICAL EXPERIENCES	RESULT IF PRESENT	RESULT IF MISSING
• Positive Predictability	Sense of efficacy	Excessive need for control
• A Sense of Being Valued and Trusted	Sense of confidence and high self-esteem	Lack of self-confidence and low self-esteem
• Lasting Commitments, Safe Touch	Ability to trust and share	Inability to trust and share
• Nonviolent Conflict Resolution	Ability to find win-win solutions	Trapped in win-lose or lose-lose solutions
• World Safe for Life, Work, and Play	Ability to find pleasure and fun in work	Excessive seriousness and oversensitivity to criticism

Compare this chart with the one back in Chapter 1, and you will find them to be very similar. No surprise! The child's sense of belonging or alienation, of achievement or shame and guilt, and so on tend to become submerged over time. Yet the negative effects of missing experiences do not simply evaporate or go away. They are expressed behaviorally as, in Andy's case, an inability to trust and share. Or, in other cases, they manifest themselves as an excessive need for power and control, a lack of self-confidence and low self-esteem, or excessive seriousness and oversensitivity to criticism. All of these, as we have seen again and again, are characteristics and habits typical of codependency.

On the other side, adults who had positive experiences as they were growing up show a sense of efficacy, of confidence, and of high self-esteem and the ability to trust and share and to find genuine pleasure and fun in their work. All represent characteristics and behaviors of people who are a pleasure to work with, as colleagues, bosses, and subordinates. The ability to deal effectively with conflict is, of course, precisely one of the four critical problem areas we have just been exploring, so we'll have more to say about that shortly.

Every one of the four areas that present critical problems for codependents—conflict management, communications, working smart, and interpersonal relationships—has an impact on cooperation and teamwork, one of the most important positive themes of this book. While a lot of jobs do not require formal teamwork, all involve some kind of cooperation. No organization is long for this world if its employees do not work together to carry out its mission. The effect on efficiency, productivity, and harmony—on the bottom line—can be swift or slow, but it is always sure.

Codependents are always a drag on those three elements that determine the bottom line. This is not because they are bad people, which they surely are not. And it is not because they are a pain in the neck, though they often are. Even people who are not codependent, for that matter, can be a pain in the neck. Codependents damage the bottom line because they have not learned good skills for cooperation. And that lack of cooperation is a result of the cramped style, the inflexible limitations imposed by codependency. Instead of working together cooperatively, Caretakers need to control the work. Martyrs need to do it themselves. Perfectionists need to do it perfectly. Workaholics need to do it all. And Tap Dancers never really commit to doing it.

But People-Pleasers and their counterparts, the Warriors, provide us with the most telling illustration of codependency's blinders, its restrictions on possibilities. A cooperative approach to work, or any other activity, sets up a win-win situation for all participants. It requires flexibility, willingness to explore all possibilities and to adopt unorthodox solutions when necessary to achieve its goals. Warriors, of course, are locked into a vision of life as one vast win-lose competition. Their personal win is what matters to them, and their running score is all they can see. Cooperation, they think, is for wimps who are afraid to keep score because they know what their score will be. People-Pleasers typically adopt a third view, lose-lose. If they do not please, they certainly lose. But so does the other person, group, or whatever—the one who is not pleased. They might like to win and wish they would more often, but their behavior is dominated by their fear of losing.

Now this is not to say that competition has no place in the world of work, nor that all competitive people are codependent. Far from it! Competitiveness does have a very important role to play, both at work and in other areas of our lives. At its best, competition keeps us alert, on our toes, prepared for those curve balls that life will certainly pitch at us. But at its worst, it narrows our vision and blinds us to alternatives. It focuses us on the short-term because we do not want to risk even a temporary setback. Organizations that operate on a rigid win-lose basis risk something even more serious—playing into the hands of codependent employees and even becoming a codependent system. Now that we have examined the particular difficulties and shared problems of codependents at work, we are ready to explore more of the broader implications of codependency in the workplace, both for the people and the system.

6

Workplace
Implications

Talking about workplace cooperation and codependency means that we are talking about relationships. Focusing on relationships brings us back to some of the questions at the very beginning of this book— How good are you at relationships? And how good at relationships are those people you encounter regularly in your work life? How is this book changing your answers to those questions and your understanding of why they are so important? Remember that codependent relationships are destructive ones where two people facilitate each other's dysfunctional habits or where an individual and a system reinforce each other's dysfunctional behaviors and characteristics.

No workplace is completely stress-free. Creating such an environment is simply impossible. What is possible is managing that stress, cutting it down, and keeping it at the irreducible minimum. Consequently, it is possible to increase both the internal and external harmony that is so important to the bottom line. The best place to start is with one of the greatest sources of stress—relationships—the relationships that people in an organization have with each other and their relationships with the system itself. Threads of this discussion have been scattered throughout earlier chapters. Now we will gather those loose ends together and weave them into our overall design.

How Do Your Tapes Mesh With the Organization's?

Take a moment to think about this question for yourself. As we have said earlier, each one of us has our own tapes and our own needs. Though we rarely think about them, we take them with us wherever we go. They are a part of each of us, and most of them have been with us for a very long time. We play them whenever a situation provides the right cues to start them, often without our paying any attention to whether or not they are suitable. Actually, it is our bus driver who does not pay attention and plays them for us. We have turned over the wheel, and we let our driver choose our behavior. Yet we wonder why we seem to find ourselves repeating the same old patterns and experiencing the same problems all over again!

So, what are the possibilities when we show up at work, or anywhere, carrying all those tapes? How do people's own tapes combine with those of the system they work in? And what kinds of relationships do they promote—healthy ones where people and the system nourish each other, or dysfunctional relationships and systems in which people are hopelessly trying to feed themselves with their twelve-foot chopsticks?

The best possibility is that our self-enhancing tapes are a good fit with those of our co-workers and the organization and that the people and the system are nourishing each other. Our self-enhancing tapes match those of others, and they all support and reinforce each other. We should all be so lucky! We all know that this happy state of affairs is rare. There are two other possibilities, the ones we are going to talk about now.

The first is that, again, we find a good fit. This time, though, it is our self-defeating tapes that match and are reinforced. We like to think of this kind of situation as our tapes meshing *too well*. The second, of course, is a bad fit—when our own tapes do not blend well with those of the organization or our co-workers.

When Your Tapes Mesh Too Well

Some of our friends provide fine illustrations of what can happen when people's tapes mesh too well. We offer several possibilities of what can occur, beginning with Dorothy. She has been a municipal clerk for many years, you recall, in a small town. Actually, the town is not so small any longer and is becoming engulfed by urban sprawl. Through the years, Dorothy has managed to grow with the town and the job. So far, so good. But things are getting tougher for her than they used to be. The expanding workload, to be expected as the town itself has expanded, has required more staff, and she cannot keep an eye on every detail as she had become accustomed to doing. These two problems, finding competent staff and keeping track of details, turn out to be more closely related than you might imagine, at least for Dorothy.

The main reason Dorothy loves her job and has remained in it for so many years is that it suits her personality so well. Precision and attention to detail, which come automatically to her, are absolutely essential for all municipal clerks. So long as the town and the job remained rather small, she really had no problems. For a number of years, in fact, she managed very well with just a single clerical assistant. Assistants came and went during those years, but she found it easy to keep everything under control. When computers came along, she was one of the first among her colleagues to make the switch. She took to this new technology naturally and was delighted that the computer reduced her need for additional staff.

Unfortunately for Dorothy, growth and the encroaching suburbs have overtaken her. Despite computerization, staff expansion has become essential and increasingly difficult for her to manage. Finding new people who are as dedicated as she is to the city and to the duties of the municipal clerk's office seems nearly impossible. It is true, of course, that Dorothy's standards are very high. But she does not demand more of her staff than of herself, and she makes every effort to make sure they know that. Then, on top of the problem of recruiting and retaining competent staff, the expanded work-load means that she no longer can keep track of everything herself. Absolutely every detail is simply no longer in her own head because she cannot be fully involved in every single task. Not surprisingly, she finds this very frustrating and discon-certing. She is wondering how she can continue to maintain control over everything she is responsible for, and she feels very stressed much of the time.

By now, you can see exactly what has happened. Dorothy may or may not have entered her job so many years ago as a full-fledged Perfectionist, but she certainly brought at least some of those tapes with her. Those tapes—those habits that she had already been practicing for who knows how many years—then combined with a job that served to reinforce those very behaviors. Her tapes really have meshed *too well* and produced a perfectly predictable outcome.

Elaine's situation is somewhat different from Dorothy's. In her office, as in so many law firms, it seems that everyone must be a Workaholic. At least, everyone works very hard and puts in very long hours given the expectation that they produce "billable hours." In Dorothy's case the match is between her own habits and her particular job. In Elaine's it is more than the particular job; the system in which Elaine works meshes with her own habits. Elaine works in an organi-zation in which a lot of others share those same dysfunctional habits. Her organization reinforces those habits for everyone, whether they are simply ambitious hard workers or true Workaholics who must keep busy in order to protect their self-esteem and mask their loneliness.

This reinforcement means that change, replacing those dysfunctional Workaholic habits, is exceptionally difficult. We have not yet talked much about change or ways to abandon those self-defeating habits and to reclaim the driver's seat of our own bus. Such change is not an easy goal, even under the best of circumstances. Elaine is definitely not in the best of circumstances. She is surrounded by others who also work long and hard, and she is in a system where doing so is a strong norm. Organizational norms, as we have already learned, are powerful behavioral policemen. They can rarely be flouted, certainly not on a regular basis by anyone who wants to stay in the good graces of co-workers and the organization itself. In other words, the deck is stacked against her. This is not to say that change is impossible for her, or that any attempt she might make would be futile, but it does emphasize the hurdles that may be lurking in the path of codependents who want to regain control of their lives.

For a third variation on this theme, remember how Chip got into trouble by promising delivery and installation of some new equipment on a priority basis for one of his customers. Chip is being hit from both sides. First, a sales job, virtually by definition, plays into the People-Pleasing pattern. You might say that Chip should have been dealing with these issues for a long time or that becoming a salesman may have been what tipped Chip over the line into codependency. You are right on both of counts.

Second, the push for expansion of sales by the owner of Chip's business puts additional pressure precisely on his weak link, his type of codependency. If following his natural bent and becoming a salesman have indeed intensified his

People-Pleasing habits and pushed him into codependency, this new work environment is likely to make things even worse for him. His flap with tech services may well be just the first of many more to come. The added pressure of this job could cause Chip to recognize his problem and begin to deal with it, but a negative outcome with things getting yet worse is more likely. The system probably will prove to be stronger than he is and, like Elaine, the deck is stacked against him.

In each of these illustrations, we have focused on the individuals—on Dorothy, Elaine, and Chip—and how they fit into their respective jobs and organizations. Now, let's flip to the opposite viewpoint for a quick look at those systems. Do you think those systems are healthy or unhealthy? What kinds of relationships do they foster? Do they increase harmony and reduce stress?

Dorothy's unit, the City Clerk's Office, is small but growing, just like the overall city government itself. Under the leadership of a self-enhancing city manager, a flexible and open approach to managing the city's growth has been maintained, and the staff has remained relatively small and responsive to city residents. Sometimes things do seem fairly chaotic, but the city manager regards that as normal given the town's rapid growth. Surrounded by a sea of change, Dorothy is proud that she has succeeded in establishing an island of orderliness and high standards.

But we know that Dorothy's little island is not so idyllic. She has had problems with staff turnover, problems that probably are rooted in her codependency. Given this information, plus the fact that many of the requirements of the municipal clerk's job reinforce Dorothy's Perfectionist type, we have to wonder whether or not she is able to build a healthy subsystem. We'd like to believe that she is capable of doing just that. Instead, we predict increasing collusion by her staff to avoid, hide, or deny mistakes and for more intensive efforts by Dorothy to keep her subsystem as closed as possible in order to maintain as much control as possible. Relationships between Dorothy and her staff are already troubled, and we have to wonder about relationships among staff members as well. We also must concede that stress—both Dorothy's and her staff's—is too high and harmony too low. The fact of the matter is that codependent people are likely to build codependent systems simply because that is all they know.

Law firms are not identical, but they have a reputation of demanding hard work and very long hours from all their employees. Is Elaine's firm a reasonably healthy organization full of ambitious, hard-working, self-enhancing attorneys or an unhealthy system full of Workaholics? Most likely, it lies somewhere in between, both in terms of the system and the staff. Even if the positive interpretation of her firm is accurate, it is an environment that does not help a genuine Workaholic like Elaine. And even though Elaine seems to be the ambitious, productive type of Workaholic, the fact remains that she has built her self-esteem on keeping busy and creating a demand for her contributions both at work and in her community. She really does have a problem. Her environment and the relationships promoted by that environment help her avoid facing it, facing up to what it really means for her and her life. Her system promotes her codependency.

Chip's business looked like a healthy enough system from the outside. During the hiring process, members of the sales staff that Chip met and especially his new boss were pleased with the coming changes. But the owner's decision to launch a sales expansion effort without considering its impact on his organization provides a crucial and negative clue. Codependent systems are not built only by codependent people, like Dorothy. They can also emerge because people like Chip's boss and his top executive team are not paying close attention to what they are doing and to the implications of their actions on their organization as a whole. Their failure to anticipate that increased sales would also require increased tech support is exactly the kind of failure of systemic thinking that can unintentionally plant the seeds of codependency in an organization. Relationships are stressed, as we have seen with Chip and his coworkers in tech support, and signs of an unhealthy organization begin to appear. Confusion and crisis management will inevitably result if these new problems are not dealt with openly and promptly. Add the collusion and denial that will surely follow close behind. Together these all combine to nurture those seeds that were planted inadvertently when no one was paying attention.

In the last instance we have only considered the problems arising between sales and tech support. We have not even considered the implications of the new sales push for accounting, purchasing, or any other department; but you can be sure that similar problems exist in those areas as well. Before we leave this story, one last point is worth making. A new focus on sales has magnified the codependence of Chip, a People-Pleaser, but other potential matches or mismatches come to mind easily. A manufacturer's enhancement of quality control practices could play right into the dysfunctional habits of a Perfectionist; a hospital's focus on patient-care standards, into those of a Caretaker; and so on.

The self-defeating tapes of a single codependent staff member are not likely to wreck an entire organization—unless that person is the boss. Then the situation can quickly become very serious, and we will talk about that shortly. Even one codependent employee can knock a lot of relationships askew and create a fair amount of trouble. The important questions are, first, how to deal with that one person, or the few people, whose dysfunctional tapes are raising the stress level for everyone and possibly going to impact the bottom line. Second, how to protect the organization from those few—how to keep it healthy, increase its harmony, and encourage self-enhancing relationships.

When Your Tapes Do Not Fit

When a person's tapes fit too well with a particular job or with a system as a whole, the question of what to do about this situation rarely arises. It would be better for the person if it did, for something needs to spur that individual to think about the self-defeating habits that are being reinforced in the workplace. When there is a bad fit—when your tapes do not mesh and instead clash, when relationships are "out of sync," and when the stress level is rising—the question is most likely to present itself.

What we are really talking about here is the fit between people's own tapes and those of their coworkers or of the systems in which they work. There are plenty of bad fits between individuals and their particular jobs. We have all seen such situations, and many of us have been in them personally. It is probably also true that people who are codependent are more likely than others to remain too long in jobs that do not match their skills and personalities. The problem is the person; jobs per se cannot be codependent. People and organizations or systems, as we have seen, can be codependent.

So what is a self-enhancing person, or one who is not codependent, to do when faced with a difficult organization or co-worker? There are essentially three possible outcomes. First, the person can leave, transferring to another job or part of the organization or quitting if necessary. Second, the person can tolerate the situation and make do—the "grin-and-bear-it" alternative. In the third and worst result, the person can stick with it, eventually succumbing to codependency along with the others.

The first option appears to be the riskiest, especially when quitting is the only alternative. Sometimes it becomes clear that sticking it out is even more risky—risky to one's own self-esteem and mental health if it means remaining in an intolerable situation. A couple of years ago David, a colleague, held an executive position with a large, nonprofit professional association that became racked with internal dissension among rival groups within the professional membership. The dissension spilled over onto the association's staff, interfering with work performance and fostering collusion and denial as members tried to force staffers to choose sides. Harmony was long gone from the organization as a whole. As the pressure on my friend increased, he became more and more stressed and depressed. Finally, one day, he said "enough!" and re-signed. Leaving abruptly without another job to go to was not easy, but staying in a situation that was becoming more stressful by the day was even harder.

By interesting coincidence, David's son was also going through a tough work situation at the same time. Following his father's advice, Ed adopted the "grin-and-bear it" solution and managed to last it out to a happy ending. Ed had worked for a few years, gone back to graduate school, and was excited and full of energy for his first position following completion of his doctoral degree. Trouble was, in a small and fairly isolated unit within a much larger organization, Ed found himself working for a weak, ineffectual Martyr. His boss not only had no energy himself, he also sapped Ed's, sent Ed off on useless tangents, and generally threw cold water on Ed's new ideas. Transferring to another segment of the organiza-tion did not happen to be a feasible alternative for Ed, and there weren't any other opportunities for him in the same geographic area. Ed felt stuck, but he did not give in. Instead, he plugged away and earned the respect and good will of colleagues that he was able to work with from time to time. And the happy ending finally came when Ed's boss was eased out of his job so Ed could take over and really make something of their little enterprise. Needless to say, his dad is really proud and glad that his son did not have to follow in his footsteps—quit and start over.

Finally, we come to the third possibility, succumbing to codependency or an unhealthy system. Obviously, we hope no one *chooses* this alternative. Unfortunately, some folks are unable to avoid it. As we discovered much earlier in this book, most of us have some habits that could lead us into codependency and maybe some relationships that border on codependency as well. Sometimes we are smart enough to figure out that we could be getting trapped in a self-defeating pattern and strong enough to change that pattern before it really climbs into our driver's seat. And sometimes we are more lucky than smart and strong—lucky that we do not find ourselves in circumstances that take advantage of our vulnerabilities. Any of us can be vulnerable from time to time in our lives, especially when we are under a lot of stress over a long period of time or if we are going through some kind of crisis. Finding ourselves in an unhealthy organization or getting a new boss who turns out to be codependent at a time when our defenses are already weak can provide just the push we do not need.

Then there are people who have long been susceptible to becoming truly codependent and perhaps just lucky enough not to have succumbed. Think of a person who has some behavioral habits that skirt around the edges of codependency, someone who has always been rather passive and generally prefers others to make choices for them, such as whether to go to a sporting event or to the theater. Such a person who wishes someone else would prioritize a list of work tasks to be done and would instruct "Do this one now, that one tomorrow, and hand a third off to a co-worker." In other words, think of someone who is almost a Baby looking for a Caretaker. Then imagine that person going to work for

Jan. A perfect match, you say? So long as Jan continues her Caretaker habits, it is true that she will be looking for Babies to care for. And when a potential one comes along, someone who could easily cross the line into codependency and become another Baby for Jan, the likely outcome should not surprise anyone.

Once again, let's shift our viewpoint from the individuals involved to the systems they work in. David's organization was clearly unhealthy, one of the worst organizational messes we have ever encountered. Relationships were distorted, stress was rampant, and harmony was nonexistent. It was probably for the best that he took the risk of leaving a truly dreadful situation. Though he is a strong person, it is difficult for anyone to avoid some negative effects from such negative circumstances.

Fortunately, David's son Ed was not caught in such dire straits. While we have no knowledge about the large overall organization in which Ed worked, it really does not matter. As is often the case in very large organizations, his small subsystem had a life of its own, independent of the larger system. And we do know that the troubled relationships in his little sub-unit were a direct result of his weak Martyr boss. Happily, it did not take Ed long to begin making positive changes in the work atmosphere when he became the boss himself. This turnaround was not instant. It never is. Ed's progress has been steady, both in shaking off the effects on himself and in laying the foundation for a healthier new system and more positive relationships among those who work within that system.

Finally, we are back to Jan and can apply the same rule of thumb that we applied earlier to Dorothy—codependent people tend to create codependent systems. Like all of us, they do what they know how to do. They repeat their comfortable habits and replay their familiar tapes. They handed over their driver's seat a long time ago. The worst thing is, when one of those folks is the boss, the dysfunctional habits and the misery those habits bring usually get spread around in ever wider circles and affect more and more people.

The Boss... and Subordinates

Relationships with co-workers and with the organization it-self, important as they are, often pale compared to the boss-subordinate relationship. Of course, none of us needs to be reminded of how important the boss can be—whether we are bosses or whether we work for one. And every one of us does have a boss, even those of us who are self-employed, who are our own bosses. In fact, most of us are both boss and subordinate. Obviously, this duality is true of anyone who is in middle management and of many others as well. So do not be surprised if you find yourself identifying first as one, then as the other in the two sections that follow. Also, given our concerns here, the importance of this basic workplace relationship holds true whether you are someone working for a codependent boss or you are the boss trying to figure out how to manage codependent employees or how to function in a codependent system.

We have already met a number of bosses in the pages of this book, so there are a lot of loose ends to weave together. Unfortunately, most of those bosses have not been wonderful examples. Before really getting into this topic, we ought to pause for a brief reminder. As we have seen, organizational problems can arise from a variety of sources, not just code-pendency. Likewise, not all difficult bosses are codependent, but all codependents are very likely to be difficult bosses. Invariably, they will have one or more of the four common problems we discussed in the last chapter—managing conflict, communicating and sharing information, working smart, and building and maintaining relationships. Every one of these four areas of behavior is important for anyone who is a supervisor, who manages others. In other words, for anyone who is a boss. These are critical skill areas, no matter what particular kind of work is being supervised or managed. And these are, of course, among the kinds of boss-related problems we will be considering.

When You Are the Boss

When you are the boss, for better or worse, power and status are on your side. With those tools comes the responsibility to use them effectively; being the boss works better when you are able to do so but worse when you cannot. If you find yourself in a truly unhealthy and codependent organization, chances are that your opportunities to act are severely limited. You may be able to protect your unit and your staff from at least some of the craziness of the system, but one person alone cannot realistically expect to take on a whole system. That, of course, was David's problem and, finally, the reason for his decision to quit.

Managing a codependent employee, on the other hand, presents you, as the boss, not only with opportunities, but also with an obligation to take action. In fact, failure to act shortchanges everyone—the codependent person, your other subordinates who are that person's co-workers, the organization, and yourself. Failure to act leads you into the trap of a codependent relationship, making you an accomplice in that employee's codependence. Maybe these statements are raising some questions, such as—How can I tell if I have a codependent employee? How can I tell if I am walking into that trap of participating in a codependent relationship? And, most important of all, what can I do?

The first thing to be clear about is this—whether that employee is codependent or has some other kind of problem is absolutely irrelevant as far as you are concerned. Your job is to manage, not diagnose. What is relevant is the fact that you have a subordinate whose job performance is, for whatever reason, not up to par. And what you need to do about that inadequate performance is deal with it sooner rather than later for two reasons. First, small problems are always easier to solve than big ones. Second, that person's performance almost certainly began to decline well before you began to notice. Supervisors may not always be the last to know, but rarely are they the first.

Figuring out whether you might be allowing yourself to be drawn into a codependent relationship might seem to be a bit trickier, but, in fact, it really is not. Work relationships differ in one very crucial way from family and social relationships. Clear expectations exist about what is, and is not, appropriate behavior on the job. Job descriptions are the basis of these expectations, together with such general workplace norms as arriving on time, not playing hooky, dressing appropriately, respecting the norms of the workplace, and so on. All in all, employers have the responsibility to establish performance standards and the duty to enforce them. And when it comes to the performance of a specific employee, that employee's boss is on the front line.

If these statements appear harsh, they really are not. They probably sound harsh to a conflict avoider and to a Caretaker, but they are solid reinforcers to bosses who understand that work is work. It is not home. It is not play. The best bosses also understand that work relationships need not preclude friendship, empathy, nurturance, and even fun. They also understand that the lines that must be drawn are sometimes shifting and may be hard to see. In the final analysis, those best bosses understand that playing into a subordinate's codependence is bad for that person, bad for themselves, bad for the job, and bad for the organization.

When You Work for the Boss

Now, take just a moment to think back over the bosses we have met on these pages. Some of them, especially newspaper publisher Robert Maxwell or Warren, from the high-tech engineering firm, are not the kind of people anyone would hope to work for. Among our six continuing friends, three are bosses—Jan, Dorothy, and Charles. We do not know right now whether or not any of them are working on their codependency problems. Others—including Earnie, a former Workaholic, and Tom, Frank, and Andy who have been in Earnie's support groups—are actively working on replacing their old self-defeating habits. And each can testify that positive benefits have been achieved, for their employees as well as for themselves. In any case, we are going to be talking about the whole range of self-defeating behaviors that are particularly troublesome in bosses—being indecisive, avoiding conflict, playing favorites, manipulating information, and so on.

The boss really does set the tone for the workplace. So what do you do if your boss does not create a positive environment or set an enhancing tone? What if your boss is an alcoholic, a drug abuser, or some other type of codependent? What *can* you, as a subordinate, do in this situation? Shifting our viewpoint from the boss, as in the previous section, to the subordinate changes the focus in important ways. If you are a subordinate, power and status are not on your side. Yet you do share at least some responsibility for the quality of your work life. You are certainly responsible to your employer for doing your job effectively and for your contribution to the organization's bottom line.

Perhaps the strategy most often recommended is the "grin-and-bear-it" solution mentioned earlier, the one Ed used when he found himself working for a Martyr. Just do your job as best you can, keep your nose clean, and hope for better days to come. This recommendation is hardly surprising, since both these sections—when your tapes do not mesh and when your boss is the problem—take the same point of view: That is, that you have generally self-enhancing habits, while it is the organization or your boss that is self-defeating. Sometimes, as in Ed's case, this grin-and-bear-it approach makes sense. In other circumstances, it may not be so useful, especially if the boss' problem is getting worse or has become really severe, and especially if substance abuse is the culprit.

We have not talked specifically about alcoholism or drug addiction in the workplace, though they are certainly tied closely to the problem of codependency. And they are certainly serious problems in their own right. It is generally accepted that at least 10 percent of Americans will have serious substance abuse problems at some time in their lives. This percentage suggests that all of us can expect to encounter such problems at one time or another in our work lives, whether with bosses, co-workers, or subordinates. And, sad to say, at whatever level they are found, typically these problems have not been well handled. In recent years, our growing awareness of the extent and seriousness of drug and alcohol problems and of their effect on productivity and profitability has led to significant new approaches, notably Employee Assistance Programs (EAP).

Whether the problem is substance abuse or some other codependence, what alternatives do you have besides the EAP, if your organization has one? Actually, not a lot. You might try speaking with your boss' boss, to find out whether that person is aware of the problem, shares your concern, and might see you as an ally in finding a solution. Or you might even try confronting the boss directly, making sure to confine the discussion strictly to workplace issues and perhaps offering assistance. Both of these alternatives are likely to be delicate situations. An unwillingness to pursue a serious discussion, in either case, is a clear signal to back off.

The single most important goal for you as a subordinate, just as it was for the boss in the previous section, is to avoid being sucked into a codependent relationship. Avoiding this outcome can be even more difficult when you are the subordinate than when you are the boss. As the subordinate, you generally are expected to carry out the directives of your superiors. Also, protecting your boss is a natural response, closely related to protecting yourself. In spite of these expectations and tendencies, this outcome is always going to be bad for you, bad for your codependent boss, and bad for the organization.

With this chapter and our discussions of how your tapes do or do not mesh with the norms and expectations of your organization and relationships between bosses and subordinates, we have woven in or tied off loose ends hanging around from earlier chapters. One possibility we did not examine when talking about people's tapes not fitting is what happens to a codependent in a healthy organization. We would hope that seeing different, more effective ways of behaving would open that person's eyes and would offer the kind of nurturing setting that makes change possible. How to promote change, how to make it possible is the essential conclusion we are leading up to. First, we have one last stop to make—a short look at the way our workplace habits affect our behaviors at home and at play, and the interrelationships among the various components of our lives.

7

Bringing the Workplace Home

Workaholics are notorious for taking the workplace home. Some lug such bulging briefcases that you wonder whether they have literally brought everything with them. But they are not the only ones who do this, and papers are not the only things we carry with us when we leave work each day.

Jan, for example, was already well established in her career with the insurance company by the time she married and had her children. Her Caretaker habits were equally well established. Remember, she began learning those habits long ago when she cared for her younger brothers and sisters. In her first supervisory position, a couple of subordinates with personal problems reawakened those old feelings and behaviors in her. You might say that is when her pattern was established—as she was learning supervisory skills for the first time, she was also reviving her old Caretaker skills. By combining the two sets of behaviors and practicing them together, this became her habitual supervisory style. Not surprisingly, this set of habits also goes home with her each day and guides her behavior as mother of her two children.

"But mothers are supposed to take care of their children." That point leads us to looking at this issue from another angle. The following story is about another woman—a friend who also combines a career with parenthood. Penny and her husbandand Tom have found a good balance between their professional and home lives, but it was not always as easy for them as it looks today. In particular, Penny has always been an extremely organized person, a habit that has generally served her well at work. She credits her organizational and planning skills for her many achievements and rapid rise in her company, though some among her colleagues regard her as compulsive and controlling. When their first child was born, Penny thought she was fully aware of the pitfalls of combining a career and motherhood. Penny proceeded to do what she knew best, organize her time at home as strictly as she did at the office. This approach worked well when it came to housekeeping, but she found it more difficult to keep the baby organized and scheduled to her standards. Sometimes even Tom disrupted her carefully laid plans.

In fact, it was Tom who finally began to figure out what was happening and asked Earnie for advice. Penny is a good example of someone who has some habits that could, under certain circumstances and with enough practice, cross over the line into codependency. These habits, potentially borderline at work, were distinctly dysfunctional in the home environment. Penny is also a bright, perceptive woman who was able to understand fairly quickly what was happening when Earnie sat down with the couple to talk about how they were adjusting to being parents.

Penny and Tom's story, as well as Jan's, remind us of several things. First, it is not only men who bring home and apply to their families habits that we still tend to regard as masculine, such as tightly organizing and managing a group of subordinates. Penny was astonished at the notion that she was trying to supervise and control her husband and child as if they were her employees, but she came to agree with the interpretation.

Jan's experience seems contrary to the norm, since she was a Caretaker long before she was a mother. She learned those behaviors as a child, perfected them as an adult at work, and finally took them back to her home and children. This path—from childhood home to work environment to adult home—is actually rather common, especially as more and more people delay marriage and family until their careers are under way.

The second reminder is even more important. Penny reminds us that codependent habits do not necessarily pervade the totality of our behavior and that their growth can be checked before they become full-blown codependency or behavioral addictions. You can throw that bad driver off your bus or, better yet, refuse the driver's seat to anyone who is trying to take over inappropriate portions of your life or to drive you toward the use of self-defeating habits. This assertive behavior requires a willingness to control that misguided bus driver, to accept feedback, and to take the risk that always accompanies efforts to change. And it takes help and support from close colleagues, family members, or friends, which Tom provided for Penny. As we have said before, change is not easy, but it is much easier to accomplish at an early stage.

Finally, these stories remind us once more that our behavioral patterns are an open system, rather like a large traffic circle. Streets enter and exit the circle from various directions and head to different destinations. These streets are the paths we use to learn and practice our behaviors and habits. Some are larger and others smaller, their size reflects the source of our learning and the impact of that source. Some old ones may be overgrown with weeds, since they have fallen into disuse and their source is nearly forgotten; others may be littered with the debris of false starts or failed efforts; while some that lead to new destinations may be emerging. The street leading from childhood and home is, of course, very broad and often continues directly into the adult family and home. For most adults, the one coming from the workplace is also wide, important, and continually travelled. What Penny did to solve her problem was block off a side road leading from her work to her home.

None of these streets or pathways are one-way, though some may be much more heavily traveled in one direction than the other. All carry our behaviors and habits, along with such other things as our basic values and approach to life, back and forth among the various sources and destinations. They also carry information from the many environments in which we live, new information that we can absorb and use to enhance our lives or dismiss as irrelevant. The great strength of open systems is their ability to transmit information and influence from one part of the system to another in order to promote adaptation to changes in the environment. This also makes it possible for us to replace old, self-defeating habits with new, self-enhancing ones. But facing the challenge of change is the topic of our last chapter. Now we are going to take a closer look at some of the exchanges that take place along the streets going to and from our traffic circle and the interactions that occur there.

Workplace Behaviors/Family Impacts

If codependency generally develops from habits learned in childhood, you may be wondering whether workplace behaviors are really that relevant to our relationships at home. After all, we have already agreed that we have different expectations and requirements for personal and workplace relationships. Recall the examples of Jan and of Penny and Tom, and remember that we are focusing on our habits and behavioral patterns. Some of those patterns can be both useful at work and dysfunctional at home. Dysfunctional behavior is not always codependent, but it is always worthy of our attention so we can deal with it promptly and thus avoid being led down the path of codependency.

Even with all these good reasons, can profitability and productivity, which we frequently have been discussing, be connected to our spouses and children? Of course not. But the third important bottom line element, harmony, certainly can. If we made a list of the most important elements of an ideal home atmosphere, there would be a wide range of opinions and descriptions. Yet nearly all would most likely list harmony or some equivalent such as "stress-free home life."

Next recall the four typical problem areas of codependency that are common to all six of the types—managing conflict, communicating and sharing information, working smart, and building and maintaining relationships. The first two obviously have a lot to do with harmony in any setting. The third, working smart, is usually less important at home than at work, so we will skip that one here. And, fourth, families are surely about relationships, and those closest relationships deserve just as much tending and care as work and social relationships, if not more. Since Earnie has written extensively on adult relationships in the past, we are going to focus first on parent-child relationships here, then on broader family issues. And since so much has been written recently about the work/family conflicts of mothers, we will be talking more about fathers.

Show me a family with no conflict, and we'll show you Ken and Barbie and their equally plastic children. From the terrible two's through the tumultuous teens, and sometimes even beyond, raising children provides fertile soil for conflict between parent and child, among children, and between parents. It should come as no surprise that the same person who avoids or deals poorly with conflict at work is no more skillful with the children at home. And it is here, in dealing with conflict, that our own childhood experience is especially likely to be repeated. The youngster still in us takes over the wheel of our bus and drives the way he or she learned all those years ago, just like Mom or Dad.

Remember Frank, a member of one of Earnie's support groups and a supporting player in an earlier chapter, who learned to hate conflict from abusive encounters with his father. In learning, practicing, and using behavioral habits related to conflict, Frank followed the same route as Jan—learning at home as a child, practicing and using these patterns at work, then taking them home and using them with his family as well.

It is well known that many abused children grow up to become abusive parents themselves—that child bus driver, no doubt, who still follows those old parental examples only too well. Frank went in the opposite direction, perhaps avoiding conflict in order to avoid the violence of his father. When he could not avoid conflict in his business, he simply handed the problem off to one of his subordinates to solve. Using the same behavior pattern at home, he had not been doing much better there than he did as a boss. At home he effectively left the scene, leaving his wife to pick up the pieces or solve the problem. It is hardly surprising that her resentment of this approach had a negative effect on their relationship. And as his children became teenagers, Frank's refusal to address their behavioral issues and avoidance any kind of disagreement, either with him or among themselves, did not foster the closeness he hoped for. Instead, it seemed to drive them away from him. It increased the distance between himself and his children and created tension between him and his wife.

Now, based on his success in learning new ways to deal actively with conflict at work, Frank is attempting some of these new behavioral patterns at home. He is trying to barricade that old three-point route—childhood home to work to adult home—and to carve out a new one starting at work and taking him home. Following Earnie's advice and with the support of his wife, the two of them sat down with their children recently so Frank could talk to them some about his problems in dealing with conflict, where they came from, how he had worked on dealing with them in the office, and finally, that he had figured out that he had to do the same thing at home with them. It certainly was a gutsy thing for him to do, and both the group members and Earnie were proud of him for taking that risk. Frank was really touched by his kids' response to what he shared with them and by the comment of his older son that he was being treated like a grown-up for the first time ever by his dad.

They are all off to a solid start—Frank, his wife, and their teenagers—though some of his efforts are more successful than others. During an argument with his daughter, Frank did not cut it off as he would have previously. They each stood their ground firmly, yelling louder and louder at each other until she cut it off by storming out of the room. Much to his chagrin, Frank discovered when he calmed down later that he had misunderstood the situation and that she had been right. Then it was her turn to be surprised and touched by her father's apology. Earnie reminded him that the road ahead will surely include more stumbles and potholes and that at home he will not have something as clear as that dramatic reduction in turnover rate to measure his success. Still, his willingness to have the argument, to listen—even if a little late—and to apologize was exciting progress toward real change.

Fathers seem more prone than mothers to bring their management styles home and to expect those methods to work equally well with their families. Sometimes it seems that the more successful the man is, the more likely he is to have trouble at home. By this we do not mean the problems associated with having a demanding and time-consuming job—long hours, weekend work, frequent travel, and so on—although those workaholic-type problems are certainly common and often serious. Our concern here is the problems associated with bringing home those very behavioral patterns and habits that so many of us practice and perfect at work, the skills that bring us promotions, raises, and success.

Communication patterns, especially with younger children, illustrate these problems with great clarity. For instance, a professional woman who decided to stay home for a few years following the birth of her second child, appreciated her husband's efforts to be home in time for a family dinner most evenings. But he was frustrated by his difficulty in holding his preschoolers' attention. With some amusement, she pointed out to him that he was approaching dinner conversation with his children as if it were his staff meeting, complete with an agenda of topics and adult vocabulary. This is a hard habit to break, particularly for a man who values being well organized and efficient.

A large-scale research study on the work-family conflicts of male executives and middle managers and their methods of coping with those issues included some interesting techniques and useful insights. One of them organized a role play with his family. "As I watched my 10-year-old daughter portraying me, strutting around, barking orders, demanding that everyone be quiet so that I could concentrate, I had to laugh," he said. But when he assumed his daughter's role, he felt a surge of resentment and concluded that "I needed to change some of my behavior." Another gave a briefcase to his young son. When he arrives home from work each day, father and son sit in the middle of the floor to share the contents of their briefcases and their day, soon joined by his wife who tells about her day as well. "It gets me back into their day and what they've faced," he explained.

Arriving home at the end of the work day, for any working parent, becomes a key moment in family life, a regular opportunity for taking the temperature of family relationships. In contrast to conflict management and communications habits where the traffic in behavior patterns between work and home is really two-way, most of us carry few relationship habits from work to home. As we have discussed earlier, those patterns are generally established in other settings, often in childhood, then brought into the workplace.

But there is one very important relationship element that we often bring home from work—feelings. Unfortunately, those feelings are more often negative than positive, since high stress days seem to be more frequent for most of us than days that bring promotions, raises, or other awards or rewards. Consequently, their impact on family relationships is all too often negative as well. How often have you snapped at your kids, your spouse, or even the dog after a tough day at the office? And how often do you actually realize what you have done and mentally kick yourself for it, if not go on to explain and apologize? The father who created the briefcase routine found it a good way to defuse the stress of his day as well as to develop a solid communications pattern with his son. That report mentioned another father who found careening down the block on his kids' skateboard, suit coat and tie flapping in the breeze, the release he needed.

Feelings, even more than some of the behaviors we are exploring, are very portable. That is, we rarely leave them behind; instead, we carry them from place to place on streets that are invariably wide and two-way. So it is that feelings that arise from home and family relationships accompany us to work and affect our relationships there, as well as the reverse. Most of us try to minimize any negative impact at work of what we regard as normal or run-of-the-mill family problems, just as we try to dissolve the stresses of the workday on our way home. But major problems may refuse to dissolve easily, whether they are such work problems as anxiety about losing your job or the uncertainty that accompanies a takeover or family problems like death, divorce, or serious concerns about a child or an aging parent. Serious problems like these always test our coping skills. And if they overwhelm our existing sets of habits and behavioral patterns, they can start us hacking out some new paths toward codependence.

Recognizing that these large problems are not easily banished or solved, at work most people deal with their feelings about such personal problems in one of two ways—they attempt either to hide them or to solicit support from their co-workers in coping with them. Hiding them, or adopting the stiff upper lip approach, may serve one's need for privacy or for firmly separating personal life from work life. But if the objective is to keep personal problems from interfering with work performance, the effort is probably doomed from the start. Even if someone is successful in sealing off the problem, keeping it isolated requires so much energy that work suffers anyway. And if that someone is using this approach more generally—not just at work—new dysfunctional habits are being born or old ones strengthened. Bottling up feelings, attempting to manage alone, keeping that upper lip stiff are all paving the street to Martyrdom.

Seeking a reasonable amount of support and comfort from colleagues, especially from those counted as friends, is often a more useful strategy. Such giving and receiving is, after all, one of the key elements of friendship. The key word here, however, is "reasonable." And the key question is who is to determine what is reasonable. From the employer's point of view, reasonable behavior minimizes any impact on the productivity of the person with the problem and ensures that co-workers' productivity is not at all affected. Yet more and more employers are recognizing that this outcome is more easily said than done and are creating Employee Assistance Programs to help their employees, to relieve co-workers of such burdens, and generally to reduce the workplace disruption caused by personal problems.

If bosses and workers do not always agree on what are reasonable expectations during a divorce, a child's serious and chronic health or behavioral problems, or other major personal problems, neither do friends and colleagues. One person's troubles may trigger anxieties and codependent responses from the most unexpected quarters. Support and comfort may not be offered by someone who had always seemed to be a solid friend. My friend Jonathan still remembers painfully the response he received some years ago when he confided in a colleague he also regarded as his best friend that he was separating from his wife and expected to be divorced as quickly as possible. This co-worker was almost the first person Jonathan told, well before anyone else, precisely because of the support and understanding he expected and needed at the time. But what he got was astonishment, followed by a blunt acknowledgment, "This makes me so uncomfortable that I don't ever want to talk with you about it," and an abrupt departure from his office. Jonathan survived, of course, but the friendship did not. And the workplace disruption between the two men, who had often cooperated closely but were now bent on avoiding each other, took months to repair.

Some Critical Differences Between Work and Home

Acknowledging conflict, handling it constructively, and developing solid, two-way communication patterns are among the crucial elements needed to build and maintain sound and mutually enhancing relationships. Both are essential to the intimacy and commitment that provide the foundation on which relationships are built and the glue that maintains them. In general, positive approaches to dealing with conflict are the same at home and at work—facing it promptly and directly before it grows and festers, instead of pretending it will go away if ignored or sweeping it under the carpet or trying to patch it up with a bandage. On the other hand, as we have seen, communication styles often need to be different, especially with our children. Treating our children as if they were our employees is no more successful than treating our employees like our children.

Where differences between work and home really abound is in relationship issues. The importance of feelings is given higher priority at home, and our standards and expectations regarding intimacy and commitment are greater. This is exactly where codependency is especially likely to rear its ugly head, for we have defined it as a person's unique set of patterns and habits that hinder the building and nurturing of constructive relationships. We have also observed that a particular problem of most codependents is adjusting their behaviors to the different demands of different types of relationships. Their problem is twofold—as children they probably did not develop strong interpersonal skills; and now, as adults, the inflexibility and limited vision typical of codependency inhibit their ability to begin learning the skills needed to modulate relationships.

At work, role and task requirements typically define the appropriate degree of intimacy and commitment. We expect commitment to the organization and its goals and objectives and to the job and its tasks as set out in job descriptions and performance standards. None of these require a personal commitment to the boss as an individual. Nor is the boss obliged to demonstrate personal commitment to his or her staff members beyond the normal responsibility for supervising their work performance and fostering their career development in the context of work unit goals and overall organizational objectives. Likewise, we expect only the level of intimacy—openness, sharing, giving and receiving among co-workers—that is necessary to accomplish tasks and to achieve goals and objectives productively. To the extent that personal commitments and greater intimacy do develop and promote workplace harmony and productivity, all well and good. But probably all of us have encountered situations where too much intimacy has damaged both harmony and productivity. In other words, both intimacy and commitment need to be modulated and maintained at levels appropriate to the workplace.

At home things are very different. Not only are feelings usually stronger and closer to the surface, but we also expect more commitment and intimacy from family members. Yet other and even more important differences exist as well—roles within families are more blurry and indistinct, family composition changes, and so do our standards and expectations. There are no formal job descriptions for family members to define our obligations or to guide our expectations. Even the informal ones that were based on popular cultural figures are long out of date. Our society is going through such rapid and profound changes that replacing those old models with a new uniform standard is impossible.

In the unlikely event that we could agree on revised family job descriptions, we would still find that as a society we are unable to agree upon a definition of just what constitutes a family. The composition of any given family rarely remains unchanged for very many years. Even families untouched by divorce and remarriage must reinvent themselves as they have a new baby, as another child grows up and leaves home (and these days, sometimes comes back again), or as aging parents move in with their children or move nearby for assistance and support.

Roles change, too, as children mature and become independent, as a full-time wife and mother returns to the work force, as either adult becomes unemployed, and as those aging parents become more dependent. In some families, however, the role of one or more family members does not change. Perhaps it is the child who has become the black sheep, the family member who is regarded as fragile and who is always needing special care and attention, the overindulged spoiled brat, an alcoholic, or any of our codependent types.

A family member frozen into such a dysfunctional role is also a signal that the family itself may be headed for trouble, or that it has already arrived. Families, like other organizations, can themselves be codependent. And codependent families exhibit the same characteristics as codependent organizations described earlier. Codependence presents at least as many problems for family functioning as it does for other organizations, if not more, but this is a topic large and important enough for another book. Before continuing with another type of work and family interactions, let's just note that the lack of clarity and the changing nature of family roles and responsibilities make recognizing codependency in a family setting much more difficult. Plus it is often much harder to know where to draw the line between being a responsible and responsive family member and being codependent.

At what point does the caretaking between partners or parent and child that we expect to give and receive become a self-defeating habit that takes on a life, or a bus driver, of its own? Or when and how, for instance, did Chip's efforts to please his father begin to go beyond what we all want and often encourage from our children? How much was it Chip's father who pushed his son to be responsible and satisfy him, and how much was it Chip himself striving to be more and more responsive?

Family Businesses

All this discussion about the families and the workplace and the differences and interchanges between them may make the idea of family businesses seem extremely risky, crazy, or both. Nevertheless, family businesses, large and small, account for nearly half of the goods and services produced in the United States as well as more than half of all jobs. Though the majority are small and unknown, large family businesses produce such diverse and well-known products as Johnson's Wax, M & M's, Levis, Estee Lauder cosmetics, *The New York Times*, Tabasco sauce, and this book.

Indeed, things often do become very tangled between family issues, workplace issues, and the fact that distinctions between the two are usually indistinct and shifting. In the beginning, when the business is still small and involves few employees beyond the immediate family, both are virtually sitting on top of each other in the middle of their traffic circle. As the business grows, the issues do separate, but they remain connected by a single wide freeway that often limits outside access.

Management of relationship issues always provides the key to the long-run success of family businesses or their failure. All the typical areas of potential disagreement—business development, strategy, management style, and so on—that exist in any enterprise are present in family businesses as well. But in family businesses, any such disagreements are inevitably worked out within the context of the dual relationships, family relationships and work relationships, with family members continuing in their accustomed self-enhancing or self-defeating family roles. The normal workplace modulation of commitment and intimacy is extremely difficult, if not impossible, to maintain. So the higher family relationship expectations generally dominate and often get in the way of sound business decisions. And if overall family behavior patterns are dysfunctional, so much the worse!

When a family business is started and developed over the years by one person, as is most often the case, these relationship issues usually do not emerge until the next generation enters the scene. By this time these issues include not only relationships among family members, but also those between the family and senior nonfamily employees. The initial stages of integrating the founder's children usually center on broad exposure to the business operations and can certainly raise questions of supervisory authority and performance appraisal responsibility. Ideally, this is when parent and child should begin to reorient their relationship, away from the old growing up/child-raising dynamics and toward adult styles, perhaps starting with a mentoring type of relationship. Needless to say, the ideal does not often happen. In many families where children are planning to join and eventually take over the family business, they are intentionally beginning their careers elsewhere in order to avoid some of the early awkwardness and to bring both outside experience and a degree of maturity and credibility when they do enter the business.

The real crunch point hits as the time approaches for serious succession planning and transfer of the business to the next generation. Only 30 percent of family businesses survive the transition to the second generation; and no more than half of those continue as family businesses into future generations. When this time arrives, so many successful business owners who have proudly claimed for years that they were building the business for their children simply cannot bring themselves to groom their successors and take the steps necessary to minimize estate taxes. Not only must they surrender power and lose the core of their identity, it seems as if they are planning their own funerals. Yet both of these actions are essential if the business is to remain in the family and thrive. In order to pay estate taxes, for instance, the Coors family had to sell shares in its company to the public, and the Wrigley family was forced to sell the Chicago Cubs. If most family businesses are smaller and more anonymous, the direct personal effects for those families, usually more dependent on their businesses for their basic livelihood, are often much greater.

This personal unwillingness to take the steps necessary for the future health and stability of the business is, in fact, codependence—patterns and habits that hinder the building and nurturing of constructive relationships. Here it is the dysfunctional founder-successor relationship that places not only the business, but also the life's work of the founder at risk. For some, this codependency may not be new, but merely a continuation of long-standing habits. Entrepreneurs are notorious for holding information close to the vest, promising more than they can deliver, and thriving on crisis management. Business founders also demonstrate codependent characteristics in their general unwillingness to give serious consideration to their daughters as possible successors. Even when they have proved their credibility to customers and other employees, some women still remain "Daddy's little girl" in their fathers' eyes. Research conducted as recently as the early 1980's has shown that most fathers would pass on their businesses to a nonrelative before a daughter. Christie Hefner, the successful President of Playboy Enterprises and daughter of founder Hugh Hefner, may be the most well-known exception to this reluctance. And daughters in family businesses, like women elsewhere, are often paid less than sons in equivalent positions.

For other founders—and, of course, most of them are fathers—codependent relationships with their children, their potential successors, may emerge only as the time for transition approaches. Transfer of power and status is not always the only issue. For obvious reasons, financial conservatism and aversion to risk are hardly uncommon among those nearing retirement. Handing over the business to a "youngster" with a different world view, new ideas, and eagerness to make his or her mark may seem certain to jeopardize the security the founder has so carefully planned. That the relationship between two individuals at such different stages of their lives, with such different needs could be a troubled one is hardly surprising.

So how do those 30 percent of family businesses that survive into the second generation do it? No doubt some just muddle through, weathering the difficulties as best they can. And there is probably some measure of luck, or lack of it, involved for everyone. But it is also clear that the family businesses that have grown and prospered over the long-run and through generational transfers have taken a proactive approach. They have allowed, even required, new generations opportunities to expand their experience, explore new directions, and prove themselves.

William and Gary Lauder, sons of Estee Lauder President Leonard Lauder and grandsons of founder and chairman Estee herself, have both begun their careers elsewhere, one at Macy's and the other in investment banking. J. Willard Marriott Jr., chairman and president of the highly successful hotel and food service company that bears his parents' name, marched to a different drummer than his father when he took on the large debt needed to initiate a serious move into the hotel business. Johnson Wax expanded into insecticides under the leadership of its current chief executive when he was still in his 20's and just starting out in the business. Now, he is doing for a son and daughter at similar ages what his father did for him—encouraging them to bring new perspectives and new ventures into the company.

Avoiding the traps of codependence is possible. So is escaping from them if you are already ensnared, though that is harder. In either case, doing so requires paying attention to the route you are taking and to its destination. And it requires paying attention to the relationships and exchanges among behaviors from work, home, and the various other important settings in your life. The ideas in this chapter are starters that we hope will whet your appetite for more.

8

Facing the Challenge: Change and How to Proceed

Paul, a friend, sat quietly reading a newspaper in an airport lounge one day when another man sat down beside him. Though the other man was accompanied by an entourage of several other men, he did not join in their conversation. Instead, he sat down in the vacant chair next to Paul, began fidgeting and squirming in his seat, then rather ostentatiously took off his fur coat and handed it to one of his group. Finally, no longer able to contain himself, he turned to Paul and demanded, "Do you know who I am?" When Paul replied that he did not, the man announced, "Well, I'm Pete Rose!" Paul, never much of a sports fan, offered an unimpressed, "Oh," to the famous former American baseball player and returned to his paper. Nonplussed, Rose, collected his coat and strode off, trailed by his retinue.

Paul chuckled as he recounted this story, but Rose's conduct represents a sad testimony to yet another case of

codependency. This man, possessor of all the fame, professional prestige, and money he could ever want, apparently
never had enough adulation. He was addicted to notoriety. In
an effort to feed that need, his bus driver climbed into the
familiar driver's seat and did exactly what he knew how to do
best in such circumstances—he tried to manipulate or control
his environment. He tried to force that adulation, to satisfy
the need for notoriety. When that desperate attempt failed, his
only recourse was to flee the scene. Just weeks later Rose
confirmed this interpretation when he was arrested and
charged with betting—betting on his own team, a behavior
that undermines the very foundations of professional sports.
Publicly humiliated, he was eventually tried, convicted, and
imprisoned. His reputation and career were ruined, and he
lost the certain opportunity to be elected to America's Baseball
Hall of Fame in his first year of eligibility.

Organizations, too, face crises and can be brought down
by inappropriate dysfunctional behavior. Union Carbide's
response to the lethal gas leak from its factory in Bhopal, India,
is a case in point. This corporation was known for being
closed, internally stingy with information, and hierarchical. In
the Bhopal crisis, Union Carbide's senior executives were
neither prompt nor forthcoming in their response to the
disaster and paid little attention to the thousands who died
or were maimed. They appeared to be more concerned with
the financial and legal consequences for the corporation than
with the human ones. And for the corporation, those consequences have indeed been severe. Union Carbide had to sell
off some of its most profitable divisions, notably those involv-
ing consumer products such as batteries, and its remaining
businesses have shrunk considerably. Yet today, it remains as
closed and hierarchical as ever. The contrast with Johnson &
Johnson's handling of its own potential disaster with their
Tylenol product is dramatic. Organizations, like individuals,

must exhibit openness and face up to problems. This chapter is a guide for how to do just that.

The Experience of Change

Some people are forced by circumstances to address their problems; others choose to address them for their own reasons; and some avoid facing up and changing. Organizations face similar choices. Both must decide for themselves and must carry out the necessary actions. Pete Rose publicly confessed to being a compulsive gambler and announced his intention to beat that habit. Union Carbide has closed ranks in an attempt to protect itself and the remainder of its business. It apparently has not changed at all.

Think back on your personal experiences, particularly organizational ones. Have you ever wondered why you and so many of your colleagues are still doing the same old things, despite seminars and training programs designed to change those behaviors? Why do the same things keep happening over and over again? Why *don't* things change?

There are three basic paradigms of training. The first and most obvious is to present information and teach some skills— education. If it seems like school, it should—it is! The second type of training goes a step further. Like education, it may include some information and an even larger serving of skills training, but its primary purpose is to motivate. By generating excitement and enthusiasm, it leads to transformation. Sales training is the prime example of this paradigm, but it is not the only one. As the service sector of our working world expands, the need increases to instill a service orientation among employees who are on the front lines dealing with customers. Such employees include bank tellers and airline flight attendants, gate agents, and service counter staff. Meeting and serving the public all day, every day, these folks perform not only mental but also psychological work. A new term has been coined to describe what is often the most taxing aspect of their jobs—"emotional labor." They need fairly continuous motivational training and support to enhance their interpersonal skills and buoy their spirits.

Both types of training are crucial to enable people to perform better in the workplace. But neither one addresses the fundamental personal issues that we have been talking about, issues that can be even more essential for effective performance in the workplace. The third training paradigm, by guiding and supporting personal growth, addresses the fundamental connection between who we basically are and how we perform. For those among us who are codependent, what is needed is personal growth. Growing out of those old self-defeating habits means throwing out that bus driver who is careening down a dead-end street and embarking on a new path that leads to self-enhancement. Fundamental change is required, not just education and motivation. Personal growth groups are one way to start down the path of change, a method that has proven successful for many people. It may not be the only path toward change, but education or motivational training alone will not be enough.

If nothing changes, nothing changes. Change means doing something new; it means growth. It means taking the risk of coloring outside the lines that we have drawn for ourselves, lines that have boxed us in and stifled us. Although it is the first step toward change, insight does not equal change. Change demands different behaviors. Developing new behaviors and new habits is never easy. These new behaviors and habits are sometimes frightening; they are always uncomfortable. But change is always worth the effort, and insight about the need for change is the first step. If used effectively, insight initiates the creation of a new and elevated life.

If insight is only the first step, what follows? All change requires three sequential steps—conversion, decision, and action. Conversion is a tricky word because many people confuse it with a dramatic religious experience. From our viewpoint, conversion is simply what happens when you really and truly reach the point of saying to yourself and meaning, "Enough is enough!" Insight is the first phase of a conversion experience. It may result from a rational process of figuring out what has gone wrong in your life. It may result from participation in a personal growth or therapy group, a self-help program or a mutual support group. It may even be one of those sudden blinding flashes. Whatever the source of the insight, transforming it into a conversion is the necessary first step of true change.

Conversion without decision—determining what to do next—is a wasted miracle. If conversion is the source of genuine commitment to change, the next step must be deciding how to change, what to do. At this point it is critical to understand the fundamental difference between *changes* and *change*. Making some changes means merely doing the same old things in a different way. For some, making changes is enough. Penny, the young mother we met in the last chapter, made some changes soon enough, before her self-defeating habits hijacked her bus. Yet someone else, who has become really codependent, cannot get by with simply making some changes. A Workaholic may stop lugging a bulging briefcase home and spend the evening instead with his or her family. But a Workaholic who simply comes in an hour earlier, skips lunch, or even agrees to become the assistant leader of a youth group has changed nothing.

True change is transformational! It requires breaking old patterns and habits and doing things that are really different. The Workaholic need not turn into a layabout, but he or she does need to spend time playing with the kids, relaxing with his or her spouse, and enjoying friends. The Workaholic's focus needs to shift from being totally centered on work and keeping busy to allowing time to relax or play. After the Workaholic has grown beyond the need to keep busy at any cost and has learned to feel more comfortable with new behavior patterns, leading the youth group activities might even be a good idea. Likewise, Caretakers need to let go of their smothering ways and let others take responsibility for their own lives; Tap Dancers must stop playing games with themselves and others and reveal both their strengths and their weaknesses, and so on.

The third step of the change process is action—turning the decisions that grew from conversion into reality. This step, the real test of commitment, is often the most difficult one of all. It is the hardest because not only will it feel uncomfortable at first, but it will also probably cause feelings of guilt. How can a People-Pleaser screw up the courage to say "no!" and disappoint people? How can a Perfectionist risk mistakes or allow timeliness to take precedence over flawlessness? Or how can Martyrs allow themselves to be "irresponsible" and risk yet another layer of guilt?

With practice and the passage of time, new behaviors become less strange and more comfortable. Even more amazing, the old self-defeating habits become more and more uncomfortable the less they are used. Not all of those bus drivers go away quietly. They are no happier than anyone else about losing their jobs, and they usually go kicking and screaming all the way. But the further away you get from them, the weaker and more muffled their screams become until they are finally and truly banished.

Whether they are large or small, entire organizations or subgroups or even individual work units, organizations must go through the same sequence of steps to achieve change as individuals. Let's return to Union Carbide, the corporation that did not change when faced with a crisis. That crisis was simply not sufficient to produce a conversion experience for an organization that was evidently very set in its ways. Without that first step in the change process, the decision and action steps never presented themselves. So what do you think must have happened inside that organization following the terrible events in Bhopal?

Contemplating the Bhopal dilemma brings to mind the Chinese character for crisis. That character is a combination of two others, the characters for "danger" and "opportunity." Perhaps Union Carbide's leaders focused all their attention and energy on danger—the danger to the corporation. The danger they faced was indeed great, and they had to address it promptly and effectively. But for whatever reasons, they failed to see how they could turn the tragedy into an opportunity. We can only speculate that Union Carbide was an unhealthy system attempting to remain as closed as possible even before the crisis occurred. Blinded as its leaders were, they were unable to turn the opportunity presented by the crisis into the insight that could have generated change and a healthier organization. Relying on their old familiar habits, they could see only danger, a view that served them poorly as it reinforced their self-defeating behaviors.

Skills for Success

The steps of the change process tell us how to proceed, but they do not provide a destination. They do not specify goals. Whether those goals require genuine *change* or less dramatic *changes*, each person must determine his or her own goals for a more self-enhancing life. No one else can do that for you, just as no one else can have a conversion experience, decide what must be done, or take action for you. However, we can offer a set of skills to target and develop.

There are six skills or behavior patterns that are critical for success at work, at home, and at play. Many of us, those of us fortunate enough to grow up in families that provided the essential critical experiences we discussed earlier, began to develop these skills and patterns as children. Others, less fortunate, have to begin learning them later in life. But all of us can develop them, and we do so by practicing them until they become habits that are an integral part of our behavior.

So what are these six? Two of them, being a team player and a creative problem-solver, really are skills. The other four are behavior patterns that are often regarded as personal characteristics—being loyal, being motivated for success, being willing to improve oneself, and accepting personal responsibility.

Having good *team players* is essential for any successful organization. We talked about effective teamwork in an earlier chapter, observing that it is an important behavioral norm in most organizations. The real key to good teamwork is turning disagreement or conflict into win-win situations and avoiding win-lose or lose-lose situations. People who are able to cooperate and marshall support are good team players. Even in settings where people work independently most of the time—such as Charles' medical practice—teamwork can be important in some circumstances. Charles exemplifies it in his willingness to provide medical care to the families of the other doctors, but the Martyr in him goes too far when he allows himself to be taken advantage of and when he agrees too often to be on call for the others, especially on holidays. Good teamwork is facilitating, or at the very least not hindering, the work of others and cooperating to get the job done. Doing their jobs for others, except in rare emergencies, is not teamwork; it is codependency!

Creative problem-solvers are a boon to themselves and to any organization. They are not stopped dead in their tracks by a problem. If they cannot plunge through it, they find a way around it. These folks are imaginative thinkers who are not afraid to color outside the lines. A lot more of us could join them if only we would give ourselves permission to do so. But giving ourselves that permission and learning how— and you can learn how, at least to some degree—require genuine change for codependents. They have to break out of their cramped, inflexible, closed behavioral habits. Brainstorming is an effective technique that groups and organizations often use to encourage this skill. Enforcing the rule that no idea is to be evaluated during the brainstorming session can cut anxiety and enable people to be imaginative.

Though *loyalty* is not a skill, it certainly is a consistent behavioral pattern and one that is highly regarded. Blind loyalty is certainly not what we have in mind. Rather, we are talking about responsible commitment to the organization and to its goals and objectives, loyalty that is matched by the organization's reciprocal loyalty to its employees. This loyalty seems to be dwindling on both sides, especially in the face of widespread downsizing. As employees, we not only work to earn a paycheck and other benefits, but also to contribute our skills and knowledge, to give back both to the organization and to our co-workers. In return for providing a healthy working environment and the tools and resources needed to do the job, the organization is entitled to expect competence, loyalty, and the other skills and characteristics discussed here, not the dysfunctional habits of codependency. Overpromising is a particularly common trap into which both individuals and organizations fall in the name of misguided loyalty. Chip's efforts to please his customers and gain their loyalty and to please and obtain the loyalty of his new employer serves as an example. Overpromising is a typical characteristic of unhealthy organizations. Carried too far and carried on too long, overpromising usually backfires. Instead of building loyalty, it breeds distrust and cynicism, which in the end destroy loyalty.

The positive elements of people who are *motivated to succeed* serve them well, and these employees can also be counted on to serve their organizations well. These are proactive people who have learned to see opportunity, to seize it, and to follow through. They are usually very competent and have no internal obstacles to hinder their progress. They are not tangled up in guilt and worry like Martyrs, who fear success. Neither are they Procrastinators, the mirror image of Martyrs, who fear failure, or Perfectionists, who fear mistakes. They are willing to fail or make mistakes because they know success requires some risk and they believe the prize is worth it. Yet like so many of the behavior patterns examined in this book, motivation to succeed carried too far can lead down self-destructive paths. Keep it in check and link it with other skills and behavior patterns on this list, notably being a good team player and accepting personal responsibility, and you have a winning combination. Give it free reign without the balance provided by the other characteristics, especially responsibility, and the price it exacts can be very high.

Willingness to improve oneself is essential to a self-enhancing life. Life is a journey of continuous learning—flexible, open to new experiences, and responsive to change. It is based on the understanding, at some level, that our lives are open systems. Sadly, these self-enhancing patterns are very difficult for codependents because they lack that basic understanding of the desirability of change. Or if they are at least somewhat aware of it, they are unwilling or unable to chance living their lives in such an open fashion. They are spending—wasting— too much of their energy on keeping their lives closed and under tight control. Dorothy is a prime example. She would disagree and point out that she was quick to learn about computers and to automate her municipal clerk's office, but her response underscores her lack of awareness. Computerizing helped her to keep control, to maintain her tidy, well-ordered little island safe from the confusion of the rapidly growing city around her. At least for a while it protected her from more fundamental change.

Last we come to *personal responsibility,* which is the keystone of our philosophy. We will talk more about this in personal terms shortly. In the workplace, personal responsibility is the willingness to act and the ability to solve problems. Rather than sitting by passively on the sidelines, a person with this characteristic sees what needs to be done and does it. This pattern is related to creative problem-solving, where the key word is creative, but the two are not identical. Here the key is initiative—the willingness and ability to act.

Jack, our Tap Dancer, provides a good illustration. As a talented designer, he is certainly creative in his work, in solving design problems; as a Tap Dancer, he always holds back personally. Because he does not pay a lot of attention to what is going on around him, he rarely sees what needs to be done. Even when he does see, his unwillingness to risk commitment stifles any initiative he might have. Jack could be a real asset to any design group, but his value remains limited.

It is probably unlikely that any one individual will have developed all six of these skills and behavior patterns to an equally high level, but most successful people demonstrate all of them to at least a moderate degree. All of them are surely important and self-enhancing goals to aim for as we strive to build healthier lives.

Building a Healthier Life

The bottom line for a healthy life is a healthy body and happy, successful relationships. We have focused in this book on workplace relationships with coworkers and with the organizations in which we work. But we have also recognized that much of what we have said applies to family and social relationships as well, for all of these parts are interlocking pieces of the total system of our lives. No portion exists in isolation, unaffected by what is happening in the other segments of our lives. We carry our behavior patterns and habits, self-enhancing or self-defeating, back and forth among these segments.

Leading the pack of self-defeating behaviors are those we call codependent. A destructive lot, they damage all our relationships, and they damage the organizations we work for by reducing productivity, efficiency, and workplace harmony. Just as a healthy body and relationships are the bottom line for a healthy individual life, these three—productivity, efficiency, and harmony—are the bottom line for healthy organizational life. No organization can survive, let alone thrive, without all three. Successful working relationships are certainly the key to harmony in an organization, and they are important contributors to productivity and efficiency as well.

Doubtless everyone is affected by codependency—at least to some degree. Even those of us who are not codependent ourselves work, live, or play with people or organizations who are. One way or another, we all must struggle with it. If you are one of the lucky ones who grew up supported by positive critical experiences and who learned self-enhancing behaviors along the way, we hope you have still found things to learn here, especially some real understanding of those who have not been so fortunate. If you are not one of those lucky folks, we hope you have found the inspiration and insight you need to begin the change process for yourself.

Back in the Introduction we laid out four points that contain the key to success in coping with self-defeating behaviors and unsatisfying relationships. Now we need to go back to those four points to see what we have been able to do with them. They are as follows:

- Grasping the patterns of dysfunction

- Identifying the present consequences of those patterns

- Understanding that healthy functioning is the goal, that it is possible, and that this is each person's own responsibility

- Building a support system to meet that challenge

The first two, understanding those dysfunctional patterns and identifying their consequences, are really what this book is all about. These promote the insight that can lead to conversion and begin the process of true change. The underlying theme—and we hope it has been loud and clear—is that we can change, we can build healthier and more satisfying lives, *if* only we will take personal responsibility for doing so. That can be a big if, because we are not promising that taking charge and changing is easy. Far from it; it is a daunting undertaking. Yet it is unquestionably worth the effort. Just ask people who have accomplished it. Then look at the elation on their faces and listen to the joy in their voices as they tell you how they did it.

Henry Ford is said to have observed, "Whether you think you can, or you think you can't—you're right!" He really hit the nail on the head there. Simply thinking we can change is not enough for most of us. Change is too difficult to undertake alone. That is why we need the fourth point—building a support system to help meet that challenge. Support systems take a lot of forms, and many people will use more than one. The first line of support consists of those nearest and dearest, right? Well, maybe. For many, family and close friends are an invaluable source of support that they could not do without. Now they become the lucky ones.

Others are dismayed to discover that some of those closest to them are less than enthusiastic, or even downright hostile. Think about it for a minute and you will figure out what is happening. Imagine all those Babies left to fend for themselves when their Caretaker says "Enough!" Or consider the shock of someone hearing a People-Pleaser say a firm "no" for the first time. Even the family members of a Workaholic, complaining for years about that loaded briefcase and no time spent with them, will have some major readjusting to do when he or she rejoins them. After all, the person who decided to change probably did not ask others' permission. Now, like it or not, they will have to change too. These people are as likely to include coworkers and close colleagues as well as family members.

Even with support from family members and close friends or co-workers, other sources of support are often helpful. Those closest to you bear the brunt of your struggle to change. At the same time, they are changing themselves and adjusting to the new you. Various kinds of groups offer support and assistance. The one that is right for you is ready and waiting. It will not only give you some new and different viewpoints, but it also will give some relief to those closest to you. Personal growth groups or therapy groups suit some people. Others are more comfortable in self-help groups or mutual support groups. Although the latter groups are similar and are usually less formal or structured than personal growth or therapy groups, there are some important differences between them.

Mutual support groups are usually intended to help people through a specific life crisis such as the death of a spouse or how to cope with a particular chronic or long-term illness. They do not deal with the kind of personal change we are talking about here. They offer advice and the opportunity to share similar experiences but not specific behavioral programs. And they expect members to leave the group and continue with their lives once the crisis has passed. In contrast, the prototypical self-help group is Alcoholics Anonymous, which prescribes a strict behavioral program and teaches that alcoholism (or codependency or whatever) overrides all aspects of members' lives and that true recovery is never possible. For this reason, leaving the group and the continuing support it provides is usually actively discouraged. There are variations on this theme, of course, but the theme itself generally remains constant.

A Final Update on Our Six Friends

What are the prospects for the six people we met at the outset of this book? Let's look in on them briefly.

We can report some good news about Jan, though things got fairly dicey for a while. Her unit was the least productive one in the division and her manager had just given her an ultimatum—do whatever she had to do with her people to meet her quotas and deadlines within six months, or else. Though she received some useful suggestions and support from her manager, she was extremely stressed. She tried to be as tough as she could with her staff, but she knew she was not very effective. Soon Jan started suffering from headaches, had more and more sleepless nights, and, not surprisingly, found herself increasingly short-tempered. After several weeks of this, Jan finally decided to seek help from her company's Employee Assistance Program. That move turned out to be the best thing she could have done, for she found a counselor who helped her to look at her management style and the implications of her caretaking behavior. Though Jan is not out of trouble yet both her relationship with her staff and her future with the insurance company now look much brighter. We cannot report that she has transferred any of her new insights or behaviors to her home life. Only time will tell—

coupled with more practice at work, insight into her caretaking patterns with her children, and commitment to change.

Chip's situation remains problematic. The office equipment business that he joined is actually in better shape. The owner began to realize the impact of his new sales push on tech support, and on other departments as well, and recognized that the various components of the business were increasingly out of balance. He hired a consultant who helped businesses in trouble, fortunately before things got too bad. The consultation included a series of team-building sessions to address interdepartmental issues, particularly the troubles between sales and tech support. The good news is that the consultation as a whole—strategic planning with the top management team and the interdepartmental team building— had a dramatic effect on the business. Paying attention to its developing problems and dealing with those problems promptly and effectively have checked the organization's growing unhealthiness. As for Chip himself, the outlook remains cloudy. The team building sessions gave him some insight into his own behavior. He has begun to grasp the patterns and consequences of his dysfunctional habits, but he has not yet turned his insight into conversion, let alone decision and action.

With Charles, we have a genuine success story. His insight and conversion experience came as a result of his son's twelfth birthday. Charles' wife had already been complaining about his willingness to bail out his colleagues at the expense of his family. It was Linda, in fact, who pointed out to him that their son was now the same age that Charles had been when his father was killed in the accident. "Do you want to miss out on the rest of your children's lives as surely as he missed out on your sisters' lives and yours," she asked, "even if you are alive?" Her challenge haunted him for days. The answer was obvious to him, but the solution was not. Yet soon he was able to talk about it more with Linda. She was willing to help him look at his priorities and his feelings and to listen to him when he felt guilty about saying "no" to the others in his practice. She was, in other words, willing to be his support system if he would make the decision to change and act on it. Explaining to his colleagues was difficult for Charles. He wasn't able to do that until long after they had noticed and begun to comment among themselves that he was changing. Again, it was Linda who convinced him that he really should raise the subject at the monthly meeting and explain both his insight and his commitment not to abandon her and their children as he had felt abandoned. He also understands how lucky he is to have found someone as insightful and supportive as Linda.

Dorothy, sad to say, has fulfilled the prediction that problems occur when peoples' tapes and their jobs mesh too well. As the city's growth continued, the city manager determined that a major reorganization of the municipal government was necessary. Though the reorganization was indeed needed, it presented him with the opportunity to deal with several thorny personnel issues. You will not be surprised to learn that one of those issues was Dorothy. It had become clear both to the city manager and the city council that Dorothy's job exceeded her grasp. In some ways, notably computerizing her office, she had grown along with the town and her function; but in others, such as managing a larger operation and staff, she simply had not. Despite his best efforts, which included sending her away to some professional development courses, the city manager had not been able to foster the personal growth she needed. She really is a codependent person who has created a codependent system. She had little or no insight into herself or the problems of her office. Without that insight she simply was not able to comprehend the basis of her own behavior or its impact on her subordinates and the system she has so proudly built. In the end the city manager finally gave up on her, the city council swallowed hard when dealing with a long-term and loyal employee, and Dorothy was obliged to agree to early retirement. Without much family, she lavishes attention on her cats, her rose garden, and her few friends.

Elaine's situation at this point is not so unhappy as Dorothy's, but her long-run outlook is not much more satisfactory. Elaine is a prime example that, "If nothing changes, nothing changes." Nothing has changed for Elaine, nor is there much prospect that anything will. She seems to be set in her Workaholic ways in her typically hard-working law firm, shoehorning in a variety of community activities and occasional family and social events around the edges. Elaine is, we should add, genuinely fond of her nieces and nephews and sometimes even allows herself to envy her brothers and their families. Still, as a result of her community activism, she has a well-earned reputation for dedication and service and has recently been approached about running for a political office. Elaine seems ready to rise to that challenge. She is, after all, one of those Workaholics who has both a high need for achievement and the ability to realize that need. In addition, she has the support of a family who is very proud of her and her accomplishments and of colleagues who encourage her political aspirations. All in all, it is very hard to imagine a set of circumstances that would present Elaine with the insight and conversion that Charles experienced or with a sad resolution such as Dorothy's.

As before, we end with Jack and with what appears to be turning into a happy ending. The key to Jack's insight and conversion experience was his renewed contact with one of his former teachers, a contact that quickly evolved into a solid mentoring relationship. Nick had been recruited by a very successful design studio just a few weeks before Jack surfaced.

At loose ends as usual, Jack heard about Nick's new position and dropped by to see him one day. Nick's pointed response was direct and, to say the least, unnerving, "I'm really delighted to see you, Jack, for you were one of the best students I ever had. But what have you done with your talent? Nothing!" But then he went on to offer Jack a job, provided Jack would not only work hard but also be willing to consider a long-range commitment to this studio and collaborative working relationship. Of course, this type of offer was just the sort of thing that had always caused Jack to flee in terror. Yet he did stay and talk with Nick for a long time that afternoon and, in the end, agreed to think about what Nick had said to him. After a week of conversations with Nick, some good times with his old friends, and a few misgivings, Jack accepted Nick's offer. The night before, they had a very long and serious conversation in which Jack shared some of his family history and his misgivings. He promised that he would come to a decision the next day and that, if he said yes, he really would commit to the new job in full good faith and face up to his personal issues around commitment. The first few months have not always been easy for Jack, or for Nick for that matter, but Jack is beginning to find some real rewards emerging from this new professional commitment. And Nick has found that he has an ally—Jack also has maintained the longest romantic relationship of his life with a woman he met soon after accepting the job with Nick.

What Next for You?

Once when I was feeling really low a good friend reminded me that "There are no endings. The end of something is just the opportunity for a new beginning." Those two simple sentences lifted my spirits, not only at the time, but for days and weeks to come. Opportunity, you see, does not always wait until a genuine crisis occurs to present itself. Yet it often does come when we least expect it. Sometimes it is easy to recognize, but at others it comes disguised, or when we are too distracted to notice. We need someone, or something, to prod us to attention, like my friend. Always opportunity presents the question, "What next?"

This question is my prod, my challenge to you. It is a question filled with hope and with wondering. We hope this book has offered you some insights and understandings that you can and will use in your work life, and in the other aspects of your life. You can use those new insights and understandings in many ways and for many results. Use it to build a healthier organization, one with a healthier bottom line. Fire the bus driver who is taking you down roads that you did not choose. Repair damaged relationships that are jeopardizing the harmony in your workplace or hindering your own performance and that of others. Use your knowledge to help you get through the rough times that surely lie ahead if you accept the challenge to change.

Codependence cannot survive on its own. It wants desperately to be fed, for it is very hungry and needy, but it does not feed or nourish others. It does not give, it only takes. So in time it will no longer receive food and will wither and die. We hope that you will carry with you the wisdom of the Chinese sage who explained that heaven is where people feed each other. We hope you will find that heaven and thrive there.

And most of all, we hope that you are driving your own bus!

Index

Abusive relationships, 33. *See also* Child abuse.
Action, role in change, 154
Activity, as a habit, 9, 18
Adulation, need for, 149-150
Alcoholics Anonymous, 163
Alcoholism, 1, 41, 127
  effect on children, 94
Anger, coping with, 25
Anxiety, in Tap Dancers, 38
Assertiveness, 131

Babies, 32, 78
Behavior addictions, 1-2
Behavior patterns, 29-48
  as open systems, 131-132
Behaviors
  learning, 12-15
  relationship to organizations, 11-12
Bosses, self-defeating behaviors in, 126-128
Boss-subordinate relationships, 123-128
Brainstorming, 157

Caretaker-Baby relationship, 32, 78
Caretakers, 30-32
  effect on the home, 129-130
  as team workers, 45-46
  in the workplace, 75-78
Catholic Church, as a system, 58
Change
  dysfunctional aspects of, 65-67
  experiences of, 151-155
  in open systems, 55
  steps in, 152-154
Chemical dependency, 1
Child abuse, 25, 134
Childhood
  critical experiences in, 23-27, 106-109
  learning in, 41-42
Children
  effect of healthy families on, 22-27
  valuing of, 23-24

Choice, versus habit, 15-16
Closed systems, 3, 54
Codependency. *See also* Workplace codependency.
  cycle of, 43
  defined, 2
  in families, 142
  immaturity and, 50
  limiting aspects of, 92-93
  magnitude of the problem of, 5-6
Codependent behavior, 1-2
Codependent employees, managing, 124-125
Codependent habits, changing, 131
Codependent relationships, 1
Codependents
  effect on efficiency, productivity, and harmony, 108
  productivity of, 74
  themes among the types of, 92-106
  types of, 30-39
Codependent systems, 3-4
Commitment, 24-25
  avoidance of, 55-56
  at home versus work, 140-141
  among Tap Dancers, 38
  in work relationships, 104-106
Communication
  in the home, 136-137
  in organizations, 98-101
Competition, 109
Confidence, building of, 24
Conflict
  coping with, 78-79, 93-98
  in the family, 133-135
  fear of, 95
  nonviolent resolution of, 25
Conformity, organizational, 61
Control issues, 31
  of Caretakers, 75-77
  conflict and, 96

in organizations, 64, 99-101
Conversion, role in change, 153
Cooperation, in the workplace, 45-48
Co-workers, support from, 138-139
Creative problem-solvers, 156-157
Crisis, support during, 162-163

Decision making, 153
Delegation skills, 76
Dependency issues, 31
  for Tap Dancers, 51-52
Drug addiction, 127
Dysfunctional behaviors, 1-2
Dysfunctional habits, 12, 14. See also
  Habits.
  in the home, 129-132
  replacing, 21
Dysfunctional organizations,
  characteristics of, 64-68

Emotional dishonesty, 33
"Emotional labor," 152
Employee Assistance Programs (EAP), 127,
  139, 163
Employee terminations, 4, 11
Entrepreneurs, 145
Everyday life, relationship of habits to, 19
Excellence, commitment to, 9-10, 19-20
Executives, work-family conflicts of, 136
Expectations
  job-related, 125
  organizational, 59-61
  in the workplace, 52-53
Experiences, in healthy families, 22-27

Families
  changing composition of, 141-142
  codependence in, 3, 142
  impact of work stresses on, 137-138
  as the origin of habits, 22-27
Family businesses, 143-147
  transfer of, 144-146
"Fathering" behavior, 9
Fathers, management styles of, 135-136
Feelings
  changing, 21-22
  impact on the family, 137-138

place in the home, 137, 141
Focus, lack of, 101, 102
Ford, Henry, 161
Formal systems, 58
Freud, Sigmund, 49

"Grin-and-bear-it" solution, 120-121, 126-
  127
"Guardian," defined, 21
Guilt, 34
  in Martyrs, 80, 81

Habits. See also Dysfunctional habits; Self-
  defeating habits.
  characteristics of, 15-19
  functions of, 19-22
  giving life to, 17-18
  learning, 12-15
  origin of, 22-27
  systems of, 18-19
  in the workplace, 44-48
Harmony
  at home, 133
  in the workplace, 91-92
Health, working toward, 159-163
Healthy relationships
  characteristics of, 2
  steps in building, 5
Hefner, Christie, 145
Home environment, 22-27. See also Families.
  effect of workplace on, 129-147
Human systems, 57, 58, 74

Informal systems, 58
Information-sharing, organizational, 98-101
Insight
  about dysfunctional patterns, 161
  role in change, 152
Interpersonal skills, 51
Intimacy
  fear of, 87
  at home versus work, 140-141
  in work relationships, 104-106

James, William, 15
Japan, work patterns in, 63
Johnson & Johnson Corporation, 150-151

Lauder, Leonard, 146
Learning
  of behaviors and habits, 12-15
  influences on, 27
Loneliness, in Workaholics, 35, 86
Love, need for, 16, 41
Loyalty, 157

Management styles, effect on the home,
  135-136
Marriott, J. Willard, Jr., 146
Martyrs, 33-35
  as team workers, 46
  in the workplace, 80-81
Maturity, 49-50
Maxwell, Robert, 77
Modeling, 14
  in children, 41
Moore, Linda, 92-93
Morality, habits as defining, 20

Normality, habits as defining, 19-22
Norms, organizational, 59-61, 115

Open systems, 3, 55
  communication in, 99
Organization, lack of, 103
Organizations. *See also* Systems.
  benefits of, 62
  change in, 154-155
  communication in, 98-101
  conflict management in, 96
  dysfunction in, 150
  healthy, 160
  healthy versus unhealthy, 61-68, 116-119
  relationships in, 11-12
  sources of problems in, 73
  structure of, 54-68
  as systems, 57-59

Parents
  reinforcement by, 44
  role in the codependency cycle, 43
Patterns
  in behaviors and relationships, 11-12
  habits as, 13
  recognizing, 48

People-Pleasers, 32-33, 109
  conflict and, 93-94
  relationships with, 117-118
  tapes associated with, 115-116
  as team workers, 46
  in the workplace, 78-79
Perfectionists, 36-37, 45
  relationships with, 116-117
  tapes associated with, 113-114
  as team workers, 47
  in the workplace, 82-85
Personal growth, 152
Personal problems, effect on the
  workplace, 138-139
Personal responsibility, 159
Pollyannas, 84-85
Positive predictability, 23, 76
Procrastinators, 81
Productivity, conflict avoidance and, 97
Protestant work ethic, 44
Punishment, in systems, 56

Reality, habits as defining, 19-22
Reinforcement, 13-14
  by parents, 44
Rejection
  avoidance of, 39
  fear of, 87-89
Relationships
  building and maintaining, 104-106
  in family businesses, 143-144
  home versus workplace, 139-143
  in organizations, 11-12
  with Perfectionists, 37
  as a source of stress, 111
  with Tap Dancers, 38
Relaxation, Workaholics and, 35-36, 42
Repetition, of behavioral patterns, 12-13, 17
Rewards, in systems, 56
Rose, Pete, 149-150

Safe settings, importance of, 25-27
Scripts, 39-41
  in the workplace, 51
Self-defeating behaviors, 16
  in bosses, 126-128

coping with, 161-162
Self-defeating habits, 29
  origins of, 41-44
  types of, 30-39
  in the workplace, 44-48
Self-defeating tapes, meshing of, 113-119
Self-enhancing behaviors, 42
Self-esteem
  building of, 23
  in Perfectionists, 82
  in Workaholics, 36, 86
Self-examination, 4
Self-help groups, 162-163
Self-image, of Caretakers, 31
Self-improvement, 158-159
Self-understanding, 7
Shadow codependency, 5
Sociotechnical systems, 57, 74
Strengths, in the workplace, 50
Stress management, 111
Subconscious, function of, 21
Substance abuse, 127
Success, 49
  fear of, 34, 80
  motivation for, 158
  skills for, 155-159
Support groups, 162-163
Support systems, 161-163
Systems. See also Organizations.
  codependency in, 3-4
  consistency in, 56
  defined, 54
  dysfunction in, 55
  of habits, 18-19
  healthy versus unhealthy, 61-68, 116-119
  norms, values, and expectations in, 59-61

Tap Dancers, 38-39, 42-43
  as team workers, 47-48
  in the workplace, 87-89
Tapes, 39-41
  clashing of, 119-123
  meshing of personal and organizational, 112-123
  in the workplace, 51
Team players, importance of, 156

Teamwork, 108
  as an organizational norm, 61
  in the workplace, 45-48, 105
Technical systems, 57
Therapy groups, 162
Touching, safe, 24-25
Training, paradigms of, 151-152
Trust, in the family, 23-24

Union Carbide Corporation, 150, 154-155

Values, organizational, 59-61
Violence, 25
  on television, 27

Walt Disney organization, 60
Warriors, 79, 109
Weaknesses, in the workplace, 50-51
Women, in family businesses, 145
Workaholics, 9, 18, 19, 35-36, 42, 44-45
  organizational encouragement of, 63
  relationships with, 117
  tapes associated with, 114-115
  as team workers, 46-47
  in the workplace, 85-87
Working smart, 101-104
Workplace, 49-69
  benefits found in, 53-54
  codependency issues in, 91-109
  differences from home, 139-143
  effect on the home, 129-147
  personal contributions to, 50-53
  socializing in, 62-63
  types of problems in, 8-11
Workplace behaviors, impact on the family, 132-139
Workplace codependency, 71-89
  coping with, 119-123
  importance of, 72-75
  succumbing to, 121
Worry, 34